When Ye GIVE

Cover art work by Nick LeGuern.

All scripture quotations are from the King James Version of the Holy Bible. *Italicized words are for author's emphasis only.*

When Ye Give by Joy Haney
Published by Radiant Life Publications
© 1992

Printed in the United States of America.

ISBN 1-880969-01-7

ACKNOWLEDGEMENTS

Thanks to Nick LeGuern for his superb art work.

Thanks and appreciation to Brent Regnart for his excellent editorial work.

Also to Kevin and Pam Seibold for their help in proofreading, their support, and encouragement to me.

A great big "thank you" to Ralph Gresham who so willingly agreed to do the special calligraphy work found throughout the book.

On Sunday, August 2, 1992, this book was finished, and Rev. Charles Mahaney preached a message at our church. During the message, he referred to Deuteronomy 26, and the Lord impressed me to include this in the book. The strange thing was that he was talking about the Acquisition of the Blood, and it really did not go with the message exactly. Oh, it went, but I felt like God had him say it just so every reader could be blessed with this knowledge. Thank you, Brother Mahaney for being a willing vessel.

God wanted this in the book, and because of your sensitivity, it is there.

Can I ever write a book without thanking my understanding husband? He graciously understands by now that there are times when the Lord's spirit moves upon me and flows with inspiration through my mind, heart and hands. He encourages and supports me, and is patient and kind; for this I am thankful.

This book came into being by several factors. The Lord ordained it, but there were several people that encouraged me to write it. I thank Mary Wallace, Revs. Randy Boling, Marvin Curry, and Robert Fuller for their encouragement to do it.

Lastly, I want to give honor and appreciation to my father and mother who taught these principles to me as a child. They were the greatest givers I ever knew. They started their marriage without the Lord, and did not have much. Their life was totally changed when they met Jesus. The Word of God was precious to them, and they obeyed every commandment. Now they have everything anybody would want. My mother is in heaven, but my father could write a book telling you about all the spiritual and natural blessings the Lord has heaped upon him as a result of obeying the principles of giving properly.

DEDICATION

This book is dedicated to a man I met when I was about twelve years old. He impressed me at that time as someone who was very enthused and absorbed in what he was doing. He was a young preacher and seemed to be everywhere at once. I remember that one old-timer called him a "whirlwind for Jesus."

I have observed this man through the years and the first impression he gave me was mild compared to the drive and consistent giving he has portrayed. I have watched him literally pour himself, his time, his money, his family, his interests, everything he owned into the Kingdom of God. He seems to be plugged into a consistent electrifying wave of inspiration and divine inner strength that enables him to give beyond human understanding.

Because of his giving attitude the church God has allowed him to pastor has grown beyond imagination. He has never failed to help anyone who asked for his help. He continually gives to the lonely, brokenhearted, or anyone that has a need. He has a wealth of knowledge, and it has been said that he has the wisdom of Solomon, the power of Elijah, and the meekness of Moses.

Much more could be written about this humble servant of God, but it is to this man that I dedicate this book. He is one of the great givers of this generation. The reason I can honor him is because he has honored God and put Him first in everything he does. This giver is my husband, Kenneth Haney, who has inspired me many times. May the blessings of the Lord continue to rest upon him as he continues to give to his family, others, and the LORD.

PREFACE

This book is the third in a series on the three principles Jesus dealt with in Matthew 6. He talked about giving, praying, and fasting. The books, *When Ye Fast* and *When Ye Pray* have already been written and published. This is the third one, *When Ye Give*.

Jesus said, "When thou doest alms, let not thy left hand know what thy right hand doeth; That thine alms may be in secret: and thy Father which seeth in secret himself shall reward thee openly." The principle of liberality in giving is what He was emphasizing. He promised that all three Christian acts would be rewarded in the open. These rewards would not only be given in heaven, but He promised rewards in this life.

Thoughts reap actions. Actions put in motion other acts. The law of sowing and reaping is from Genesis to Revelation. An actual account of one act reaping another act was the story of Dr. Howard Kelley. While he was in medical school, he sold books to help pay his tuition. One hot summer day he stopped at a farmhouse for a glass of water. A girl came to the door, and when he asked for the water, she said, "I will give you a glass of milk if you wish."

He drank the cool, refreshing milk heartily as they talked and became friends.

The years passed and Dr. Kelley graduated from medical school and became the chief surgeon at Johns Hopkins Hospital. One day, a patient was admitted to the great hospital. She was from the rural area and was seriously ill. She was given special care, and was placed in a private room with a private nurse. The skilled chief surgeon spared no effort to make the patient well.

One day she was told by the head nurse that she would be going home. They brought her the bill and as she looked at every itemized cost, her heart sank lower and lower. When she got to the bottom of the bill, she saw the following notation: "Paid in full with one glass of milk!" It was signed, *Howard A. Kelley, M.D.* That was an expensive glass of milk.

Just as the doctor paid her back, God pays back even more. This book deals with many different ways to give, and if the reader is willing to change some habits in his or her life, he or she will be forever blessed! One writer said, "We should give as we would receive, cheerfully, quickly, and without hesitation; for there is no grace in a benefit that sticks to the fingers."

Table of Contents

Chapter 1

WHAT DOES IT MEAN TO GIVE?

The parents of a young man who was killed in the war gave their church a check for two hundred dollars as a memorial to their loved one. When the presentation was made, another war mother whispered to her husband, "Let us give the same for our boy." The father said, "Why, what are you talking about? Our boy didn't lose his life." The mother said, "That's just the point. Let us give it because he didn't."

Giving is an attitude. You give every day. It is either a negative or positive gesture, but you do give out something. You will give yourself to many things; why not give yourself to something that will increase you instead of decrease you?

Give means to make over or bestow without receiving a return; to confer without compensation; to grant or confer; to bestow freely or fully; to devote, surrender, or apply; to yield.

When you buy something in the store or make a purchase you give money to the cashier and receive something for your money. When you give you just release the money without purchasing anything.

You cannot do anything well if you are trying to save something. If you are saving your hands, you will not do good housework; if you are saving your clothes, worrying about them, you will not have a good time. If you are saving yourself, you are holding something back.

Jesus said it this way: "If any man will come after me, let him deny himself, and take up his cross daily, and follow me. For whosoever will *save* his life shall lose it: but whosoever will lose his life for my sake, the same shall *save* it" (Luke 9:23-24). The best way to save something is to give it away.

Through Rochester, New York, runs the Genessee River between steep and crooked banks. One evening, a gentleman who lived in the city, had just arrived by train from a journey. He was anxious to go home and meet his wife and children. He was hurrying along the streets when he saw on the bank of the river a lot of excited people. "What is the matter?" he shouted.

They replied, "A boy's in the water!"

"Why don't you save him?" he asked.

In a moment, throwing down his carpet-bag and pulling off his coat, he jumped into the stream, grasped the boy in his arms and struggled with him to the shore. As he wiped the water from his dripping face and brushed back his hair, he exclaimed, "Heaven, it is my boy!" He had plunged in for the boy of somebody else and saved his own.

Giving starts with the heart. The hand is just an extension of the heart and mind. The closed fist is a closed mind. The open hand is an open generous heart. Real generosity is the surest way of thriving.

"There was a man, though some did count him mad;
The more he cast away the more he had."
John Bunyan

"It is more blessed to give than to receive" (Acts 20:35). Jesus taught the principles of giving in Mark 4 when He told them,

If any man have ears to hear, let him hear...Take heed what ye hear: with what measure ye mete, it shall be measured to you: and unto you that hear shall more be given. For he that hath, to him shall be given: and he that hath not, from him shall be taken even that which he hath (Mark 4:23-25).

Do you think this is a hard saying? Jesus explains more fully in Luke 19 what He really means. It is not God that takes it away; it is the person himself because of his lack of understanding of the principles of giving.

Jesus told the story of the nobleman who left on a journey. Before he left he called in his ten servants and gave each of them a pound and told them to, "Occupy till I come" (Luke 19:13). When the nobleman returned from his journey, he called his servants in for a report of what they did with the money he gave to them.

The first servant said that his pound had made an increase of ten pounds. The nobleman was pleased and granted him a promotion. The second came and told him that his pound had made a gain of five pounds. Again he was met with approval and received a promotion. Then one of the servants came and made all kinds of excuses and told his master that he did not do anything with the money to increase it. The master was angry and took the money from him and gave it to the one who had been a good steward over his money. He became poorer by hoarding and not giving or investing in something that paid dividends.

There is a difference between miserliness and good stewardship. Miserliness is hoarding all to self. The French millionaire miser, M. Foscue, in order to hide his treasure securely, dug a cave in his wine cellar so large and deep that he could go down only with a ladder. At the entrance was a door with a spring lock which would automatically shut itself.

After sometime, he disappeared. A search was made for him but to no avail. At last, his house was sold.

The purchaser of the house began to rebuild it and discovered a door in this cellar, and descending, found Mr. Foscue lying dead on the floor, with a candlestick nearby. His vast wealth amassed and hidden was with him. He had apparently gone into the cave and the door accidentally closed, shutting him in. He died for lack of food. He had eaten the candle and gnawed the flesh off both his arms. Thus he died in the midst of the treasure which he had accumulated, but which did him no good.

Money is not the only thing to give. Many things need to be given. The list is long and desperate. So many needs, but not enough people who are willing to meet the needs.Charles Dickens said, "No one is useless in the world who lightens the burden of it for any one else." Givers are needed in this self-centered generation. Rev. G.F. Peabody said, "The way to bear one's own burdens is to add to them the bearing of someone else's. The way out of your own trial is by entering into the trial of others. The introspective and self-absorbed sorrow grows heavier the longer you watch it, and the self-forgetting service of another lightens the burden which you yourself have to bear. The more you shirk, the more you have to bear. The more you add of others' responsibilities, the more you subtract from your own."

You multiply your blessing by giving yourself away to others. You multiply your money by giving it to God and others. Giving is the surest way to gain. It is God's master plan for the ages. The classics tell of a lake called Avernus, which means "birdless." A poisonous vapor arises from its foul waters. Birds attempting to fly across it fall stupefied into its bosom. The eagle's wing becomes powerless, and gradually the proud bird sinks down until its lifeless body floats upon the dark waters. The nightingale loses by degrees her power of song, and at length the sweet singer falls trembling into the waves of death.

This fictional story shows what happens to those who do not give. The lake is called selfishness. All who come in contact with the selfish and self-centered lake or person is not blessed, but is given a sting of death. The bowels of the person are shut up and no compassion flows to the hurting. The pocketbook is closed to God, and thousands that could be blessed by the monetary assistance of the selfish person are cast into a lake of fire. Stinginess is a stinking disease that sends off putrid odors of rotten malignancy.

The spirit of giving, which must grasp hold of each Christian, is giving to God what rightfully belongs to Him. We rob God in many ways. Dr. J.R. Miller said, "We rob God and hurt His heart every time we receive any favor at whatsoever hand and fail to speak our praise to Him."

We rob ourselves of many things simply because we fail to give. James T. Field said, "Life is a mirror, if you smile upon it, it smiles back again on you." Those who bring sunshine into the lives of others cannot keep it from themselves. Everything God created was made to give or help something else.

God made the sun. . . . . . . *it gives.*
God made the moon. . . . . *it gives.*
God made the stars. . . . . . *they give.*
God made the air. . . . . . . *it gives.*
God made the clouds. . . . *they give.*
God made the earth. . . . . *it gives.*
God made the sea. . . . . . . *it gives.*
God made the trees. . . . . *they give.*
God made the flowers. . . *they give.*
God made the fowls. . . . . *they give.*
God made the beasts. . . . *they give.*
God made the plants. . . . *they give.*
God made man. . .
                        . . . He has a choice to give or keep!

God so loved that He gave. It was President John F. Kennedy who said, "Ask not what your country can do for you; ask what you can do for your country." It is time to take on the attitude of God--that of a giver. What can I give to the Lord? What can I give to others? What can I do for my country that will make it better? How can I spread cheer to those about me? Ask yourself the questions, "What did I give today that was written down in the pages of the eternal bookkeeping system?" "Did I take, demand, or keep all day, or did I give and give until I lifted a heavy load of another?"

Section 1

GOLD

Gold represents money. Money: a medium of exchange; wealth reckoned in terms of money; considered as cash asset; anything customarily used as a medium of exchange and measure of value, as sheep, copper rings, or anything having a conventional use; any written or stamped promise or certificate, such as a government note or bank note.

One of Aesop's Fables tells of a miser who sold all of his possessions. He then made an ingot of the gold that he got for them, and hid it in a certain spot, where his own heart and thoughts were buried with it. Every day he came to gloat over his treasure. A laborer who had watched him guessed his secret, dug up the gold, and carried it away. When the miser came and found the hole empty he began to lament and pluck out his hair.

A passer-by who saw him inquired as to the cause of his grief, and said: "Do not be so downcast, sir. Even when you had the gold you might as well not have had it. Take a stone instead and put it in the earth, and imagine that you have the gold there. That will serve the same purpose. For as far as I can see, even when it was there you did not make any use of the gold that you possessed."

Chapter 2

WHY TITHE?

It has been stated by Oscar Lowery, "that if the Protestant people of America alone were tithing their income we could easily evangelize the entire world and put a copy of the Bible into the hands of every heathen on earth inside of ten years. According to government statistics, we are spending annually in this country six hundred dollars for luxuries for every dollar we spend for missions."

Sometimes we get our priorities mixed up. Some time ago a boy fell into an old well. In a short while $40,000 was raised in his small community to bring in the necessary earth-moving equipment for his rescue. In 1937, Amelia Earhart, attempting a round-the-world flight, was reported lost. For the following ten days, our government and others spent over $250,000 daily searching for her. We place highest value on this life. We spend sometimes comparatively little on seeking lost souls.

Will a man rob God? Yet ye have robbed me. But ye say, Wherein have we robbed thee? In tithes and offerings. Ye are cursed with a curse: for ye have robbed me, even this whole nation. Bring ye all the tithes into the storehouse, that there may be meat in mine house, and prove me now herewith, saith the Lord of hosts, if I will not open you the windows of heaven, and pour you out a blessing, that there shall not be room enough to receive it. And I will rebuke the devourer for your sakes, and he shall not destroy the fruits of your ground; neither shall your vine cast her fruit before the time of the field, saith the Lord of hosts (Malachi 3:8-11).

Prove me. God was so sure that His system of tithes and offering worked that He threw out a challenge to those that would try it. *Prove* means to try or ascertain by an experiment, or to test and see if something works. Tithe is a tenth of all earnings or increase.

Notice a key word: *robbed* is used three times and *rob* is used once. Four times God speaks about His people robbing Him. To rob means that you take something from someone that belongs to Him. So the tithe belongs to God. It is never man's to decide whether he will pay it or not; it is God's. God will not come down and take it out of your hand unto Himself; He expects you to give it to Him.

Notice also what happens when you pay tithes and give offerings. God emphasizes that first of all the tithe will bless His house. Then the blessing would pour out on the giver so much that he would have more than he needed. Thirdly, God himself would rebuke the devourer and keep the substance that belongs to you from decay or rot. The blessing of the Lord is pronounced on the giver in verse 12. The blessing is promised, but there has to be some giving before the blessing. Not just some giving, but giving according to God's plan.

Everyone goes through testing times, but if you are continually in financial trouble, you are not doing something right. God's word does not lie. It is as solid as a rock, as faithful as the ocean, and forever true. God will bless those that are faithful stewards and give as He has instructed to do. It is not the will of God for mankind to live in financial struggle all his life. As John wrote, "Beloved, I wish above all things that thou mayest prosper and be in health, even as thy soul prospereth" (III John 2). He wants His children to prosper financially and physically, but His first priority is our souls' prosperity.

Proverbs 3:9,10 gives wisdom and promise to everyone that will follow the Word. "Honor the Lord with thy substance, and with the firstfruits of all thine increase; so shall thy barn be filled with plenty, and thy presses shall burst out with new wine."

In Old Testament law God claimed tithes and gifts for the worship of the sanctuary and the necessities of the poor. The work of God should be provided for before man's indulgence.

All the best of the oil, and all the best of the wine, and of the wheat, the *firstfruits* of them which they shall offer unto the Lord, them have I given thee. And whatsoever is *first* ripe in the land, they shall bring unto the Lord...And, behold, I have given the children of Levi, all the *tenth* in Israel for an inheritance, for their service which they serve, even the service of the tabernacle of the congregation...But the tithes of the children of Israel, which they offer as an heave-offering unto the Lord, I have given to the Levites to inherit (Numbers 18:12-13a,21,24).

What were first-fruits? They were that portion of the fruits of the earth and other natural produce which, by the usage of the Jews and other ancient nations, was offered to God as an acknowledgment of His supreme dominion and a thanksgiving for His bounty. Among the Jews, the institution of first-fruits comprised both public and private offerings. Of the former class, there were three principal offerings. The first was at the opening of the grain harvest. On the day after the Passover Sabbath, 16th of the month Nisan, a sheaf of new grain, cut and gathered with much solemnity, was carried to the Holy Place, and there waved before the altar (Leviticus 23); nor was it permitted to commence the harvest-work till after this solemn acknowledgment of the gift of fruitfulness.

Again, at the Feast of Pentecost, two loaves of leaven bread, made from the flour of the new harvest were waved, with a similar form of worship, before the altar (Exodus 34). Thirdly, at the Feast of Tabernacles, in the seventh month, was held the great feast of the gathered-in harvest, the final acknowledgement of the bounty of God in the fruits of the year (Exodus 23:16).

Besides these public offerings of first-fruits on the part of the entire people, individual Jews were bound to private offerings, each on his own behalf.

1. A cake of the first dough of the year was to be offered to the Lord (Numbers 15:21).

2. The first of all the fruits were to be placed in a basket, and carried to the appointed place, where the basket was to be offered with a prescribed form of words, commemorative of the sojourn of Israel in Egypt, and of His deliverance by the strong hand (Deuteronomy 26:2).

Tithing was observable under the patriarchal system, in the words of Jacob. "And this stone, which I have set for a pillar, shall be God's house: and of all that thou shalt give me I will surely give the tenth unto thee" (Genesis 28:22). It was also in the offering of Abraham to Melchizedek. "And blessed be the most high God, which hath delivered thine enemies into thy hand. And he gave him tithes of all" (Genesis 14:20).

The New Testament has also its plan of meeting God's claim, containing the same elements of priority, certainty, proportion and system. "Upon the first day of the week let every one of you lay by him in store, as God hath prospered him..." (I Corinthians 16:2). Reference is made to the workers being cared for by those they served in the following scriptures:

Nor scrip for your journey, neither two coats, neither shoes, nor yet staves: for the workman is worthy of his meat (Matthew 10:10).

And in the same house remain, eating and drinking such things as they give: for the laborer is worthy of his hire (Luke 10:7).

Who goeth a warfare any time at his own charges? who planteth a vineyard, and eateth not of the fruit thereof? or who feedeth a flock, and eateth not of the milk of the flock? Say I these things as a man? or saith not the law the same also? For it is written in the law of Moses, Thou shalt not muzzle the mouth of the ox that treadeth out the corn. Doth God take care for oxen? Or saith he it altogether for our sakes? For our sakes, no doubt, this is written: that he that ploweth should plow in hope; and that he that thresheth in hope should be partaker of his hope. If we have sown unto you spiritual things, is it a great thing if we shall reap your carnal things? If others be partakers of this power over you, are not we rather? Nevertheless we have not used this power; but suffer all things, lest we should hinder the gospel of Christ. Do ye not know that they which minister about holy things live of the things of the temple? and they which wait at the altar are partakers with the altar? Even so hath the Lord ordained that they which preach the gospel should live of the gospel (I Corinthians 9:7-14).

It is God's plan that the tithe be under the authority of the ministry. They are to humbly and conscientiously be a steward over the tithes and offerings. The tithe is to take care of the ministry and the work of God.

And this shall be the priest's due from the people, from them that offer a sacrifice, whether it be ox or sheep; and they shall give unto the priest the shoulder, and the two cheeks, and the maw. The firstfruit also of thy corn, of thy wine, and of thine oil, and the first of the fleece of thy sheep, shalt thou give him. For the Lord thy God hath chosen him out of all thy tribes, to stand to minister in the name of the Lord, him and his sons forever (Deuteronomy 18:3-5).

The minister is responsible to God for how he handles the tithes and offerings. He stands in an awesome position, not only to feed the sheep, but to steward the household of God spiritually and financially. The money belongs to God, but a called man is given authority over it. It is not to be taken lightly or handled in a sloppy, unbusinesslike way. Integrity, carefulness, and sensitivity to God is required in this great responsibility.

The tithe was always given to God first. It is not man's in the first place; it is already God's. He wants you to show honor to Him by giving back to Him this small amount in thanksgiving to Him for *all* He has given to you.

The *Preacher's Homiletic* gives insight into the financial law of Christ. "Christ is sole King in His church. The constitution of the church is Christian, not Jewish. The apostle Paul was the organizer of churches, and the first epistle to the Corinthians is the great church-organizing epistle. In its closing chapter the apostle institutes a system of finance. This system bears the character of an authoritative and repeated law. 'As I have given order to the churches of Galatia, even so do ye.' The method taught by the apostle to provide the revenues of the church is an expansion of Jewish and Pentecostal church systems, an example for us, an implied and inferential obligation sustained by cumulative and presumptive argument. They appeal to a willing heart more than a legal mind. Christ rules in love, but His will should not have less authority or constraining power on that account."

All should tithe because it is God's plan. All of life, property, or money is a trust. God should be the silent partner. He allows man nine-tenths to handle his business and God's legal share is one-tenth. The only honest thing to do is to set aside what belongs to God as His share in the profits of the partnership. Nine-tenths under God's guidance and blessing will go farther than ten-tenths when the silent partner is crowded out.

Tithing is a good business proposition. God needs billions to relieve suffering and to educate children and youth. The gospel must be preached to every creature. How can this be done without money? The tithes and offerings are the stream of gold to pay these bills. When His tithe stream swells, your portion--nine-tenths--will proportionately rise, overflowing the banks and causing blessings to stream everywhere.

History has proven that those which have tithed a tenth have been blessed and those that have tithed more than a tenth have been blessed even more. Henry P. Crowell, affectionately called "The Autocrat of the Breakfast Table," contracted tuberculosis when a boy and could not go to school. After hearing a sermon by Dwight L. Moody, young Crowell prayed, "I can't be a preacher, but I can be a good businessman. God, if you will let me make money, I will use it in your service."

Under the doctor's advice Crowell worked outdoors for seven years and regained his health. He then bought the little run-down Quaker Mill at Ravanna, Ohio. Within ten years Quaker Oats was a household word to millions. Crowell also operated the huge Perfection Stove Company. For over forty years Henry P. Crowell faithfully gave sixty to seventy percent of his income to God's causes, having advanced from an initial ten percent.

Rockefeller was once asked if he paid tithes. He answered, "Yes, I tithe, and I would like to tell you how it all came about. I had to begin work as a small boy to help support my mother. My first wages amounted to $1.50 per week. The first week after I went to work, I took the $1.50 home to my mother and she held the money in her lap and explained to me that she would be happy if I would give a tenth of it to the Lord.

"I did, and from that week until this day I have tithed every dollar God has entrusted to me. And I want to say, if I had not tithed the first dollar I made I would not have tithed the first million dollars I made."

God's system of tithing works. God's work is blessed and the giver of tithes is blessed over and over again. When William Colgate was just a young lad of sixteen, he left home to seek his fortune. He met an old canal-boat captain and told him his father was too poor to keep him, and that the only trade he knew was candle-making.

The old man then kneeled and prayed earnestly for the boy and advised: "Someone will soon be the leading soap-maker in New York. It can be you as well as someone else. Be a good man, give your heart to Christ, pay the Lord all that belongs to Him, make an honest soap; give a full pound, and I'm certain you'll be a prosperous and rich man."

So William went into the city and found a church. Of the first dollar he earned he gave one-tenth to God. Ten cents of every dollar were sacred to the Lord. He eventually became the owner of the business where he was employed. He followed the old man's advice--he made an honest soap, gave a full pound and instructed his book-keeper to open an account with the Lord of one- tenth of all income. The business grew, so he began to give two-tenths, then three, four, and five-tenths; finally he gave all his income. He gave millions to the cause of Christ as God increased Him because of his modest start.

You might ask the question: "I am in debt. How can I start tithing when I don't even have enough money to pay my bills?" Let me answer your question with a story. A.A. Hyde, a millionaire manufacturer, said he began tithing when he was $100,000 in debt. Many men have said they considered it dishonest to give God a tenth of their income while they were in debt. Mr. Hyde said he agreed with the thought until one day it flashed upon him that God was his first creditor. Then he began paying God first, and all the other creditors were eventually paid in full.

Another story proves that God's system works! In the middle of the Depression when things blew up in his face, Kenneth S. Keyes of Florida, leading realtor of the South, started tithing. He gave to God not with the idea that it would help him make more money but because he believed God had first claim on his life.

As God prospered his real estate business, Keyes organized seven different corporations which sell and lease real estate, provide mortgages and manage property. In 1938 Keyes decided that his corporations would tithe also. Today the tithed moneys of all Keyes' companies go into a foundation which has a charter provision which stipulates that 56 2/3 percent of all funds must go to evangelical Christian causes.

If you withhold from God, He withholds from you. You cannot cheat God and get by. God is a good bookkeeper. R.G. LeTourneau learned this. He was an earthmoving machinery manufacturer who failed often in the earlier years of his career. One year, though, in the middle of the Depression, he made $35,000 profit. Puffed up with pride, he withheld the payment of his $5,000 annual pledge to the church in order to reinvest it in the business, intending to give the Lord an even greater share the following year when he anticipated a net profit of $100,000.

Within a year, his anticipated $100,000 profit had turned into a $100,000 loss, and brought him to his knees.

He got off his knees and pledged not only $5,000 to his church for the year he skipped, but also the same amount for the following year--in the face of a $100,000 debt and no money for payroll. From that point on, LeTourneau's fortune changed and within four years, he and his wife founded the LeTourneau Foundation comprised of ninety percent of the stocks of LeTourneau Corp., the earnings of which financed Christian work worldwide. At one time, this foundation was worth $40 million. LeTourneau often said: "It is not how much money I give to God, but how much of God's money I keep for myself."

Does this sound like the Bible story of the rich men and the little widow?

And Jesus sat over against the treasure, and beheld how the people cast money into the treasure: and many that were rich cast in much. And there came a certain poor widow, and she threw in two mites, which make a farthing. And he called unto him his disciples, and saith unto them, Verily I say unto you, That this poor widow hath cast more in, than all they which have cast into the treasure: For all they did cast in of their abundance; but she of her want did cast in all that she had, even all her living (Mark 12:41-44).

Before LeTourneau died he was giving up to ninety percent of his income to God. He went from $100,000 in debt to a profit of over $40 million by placing God into his plans. He proved God and discovered His plan worked.

Moses writes, "And all the tithe of the land, whether of the seed of the land, or of the fruit of the tree, is the Lord's: it is holy unto the Lord" (Leviticus 27:30).

Tithing is not only to bless God and His work, but it is to teach men to put God and His kingdom first. With many people, self, home, business and pleasure come first. Time, attention, energy and money are given to other things; if there is any left the Kingdom of God may get it. God takes last place instead of first. The main object, therefore, must be to reverse the order. When a man is asked to become a tither, he is asked to establish as a life principle the habit of putting God first.

Tithing is also to teach men and women to recognize and acknowledge God's ownership. God owns the property, land, money and income which we call our own. It is God's world. "For of him, and through him, and to him, are all things: to whom be glory forever" (Romans 11:36). The gold and the silver belong to Him. The first principle of tithing is not to pay the preacher, but it is to pay God what already belongs to Him. If a Christian will recognize God's ownership of the tithe, he will recognize God's ownership of all. The tither, recognizing and acknowledging God's ownership, pays his tithe from a high spiritual motive. He renders unto God the things which belong to Him. Everything comes from God and everything goes back to Him. Your financial foundation must be built on God's plan. If your system is built on your bank account, your house, or your human resources then you are not operating on God's plan.

If God is your source, you will always have enough. "The young lions do lack, and suffer hunger: but they that seek the Lord shall not want any good thing" (Psalm 34:10). Whatever the need, God will supply it, for He owns it all. "The earth is the Lord's, and the fulness thereof; the world, and they that dwell therein" (Psalm 24:1).

Tithing is an act of worship. A person's money is a part of him. When he gives money he gives a part of himself back to God. His tithe is not merely answering a temporary financial call; it is given as an act of worship. The paying of tithes causes the Christian to enter the abundant life.

So what do you tithe on? You tithe on all your increase. "Thou shalt truly tithe all the increase of thy seed, that the field bringeth forth year by year" (Deuteronomy 14:22).

And you should not just barely squeeze by, such as making sure your tithes are to the exact penny, but you should always give it abundantly, making sure God gets all His share.

And as soon as the commandment came abroad, the children of Israel brought in abundance the firstfruits of corn, wine, and oil, and honey, and of *all* the increase of the field; and *the tithe of all things* brought they in *abundantly* (II Chronicles 31:5).

The people were instructed in Nehemiah's time to give their firstfruits, their offerings, and their tithes.

And to bring the firstfruits of our ground, and the firstfruits of all fruit of all trees, And that we should bring the firstfruits of our dough, and our offerings...and the tithes of our ground...and the Levites shall bring up the tithe of the tithes unto the house of our God, to the chambers, into the treasure house (Nehemiah 10:35,37,38).

Will a person go to heaven if he does not pay his tithes and offerings? God calls him a robber if he does not. You be the judge after you read the following scripture. (All men will be judged at the end of time by the Word of God, and it is better to judge ourselves with the Word now, than to be judged when it is too late.) Paul writes by the inspiration of the Holy Spirit these words: "Know ye not that the unrighteous shall not inherit the kingdom of God? Be not deceived: neither fornicators, nor idolaters, nor adulterers, nor effeminate, nor abusers of themselves with mankind, nor thieves, nor covetous, nor drunkards, nor revilers, nor extortioners, shall inherit the kingdom of God" (I Corinthians 6:9-10). Notice God put the thieves with the drunks, adulterers, and effeminate.

The definition of *thief* is, "one who steals, esp. stealthily or secretly; a robber." Can it be said any plainer? A person that steals or robs from God will not inherit the kingdom of God, but if he gives to God he will be blessed. You alone can choose how much blessing you receive by the amount of your gift.

Chapter 3

MORE ABOUT FIRSTFRUITS

The incident of Abraham paying tithes is mentioned as a point of reference in the preceding chapter. Let us look at it more closely. King Chedorlaomer made an alliance with other kings and told the owners of the plains that they would have to pay tribute. After the twelfth year, the plainsmen said, "That's enough!" In the thirteenth year they did not pay and in the fourteenth year the King came and took the tribute money and everything else they owned. He also took Lot with him.

When word came to Abraham that his nephew had been kidnapped, "...he armed his trained servants, born in his own house, three hundred and eighteen, and pursued them unto Dan" (Genesis 14:14).The four armies had just finished whipping five kings and their armies, but the Lord was with Abraham, and gave him the victory.

When Abraham returned from the slaughter of Chedorlaomer, and the other kings that were with him, the king of Sodom ran out to meet him. Melchizedek, the king of Salem, also went out to meet him. Notice the attitude and approach of the two different kings. The king of Sodom could be likened unto the devil, and Melchizedek represents Jesus, the Almighty God.

The king of Sodom told Abraham to take everything he had for himself. First of all, he did not have the right to give it to Abraham, because he lost the battle. Everything now belonged to Abraham. He had the say as to what to do with it. The devil will try to tell you, "Keep everything you have for yourself."

> And Abram said to the king of Sodom, I have lift up mine hand unto the Lord, the most high God, the possessor of heaven and earth, That I will not take from a thread even to a shoelatchet, and that I will not take any thing that is thine, lest thou shouldest say, I have made Abram rich (Genesis 14:22-23).

Abraham wanted all to know that God was his source.

Notice that Abraham paid his tithes before he dealt with the slimy king of Sodom. In the verses preceding his remarks to the king, it says he gave attention to the priest of the most high God first. Melchizedek blessed the Lord and acknowledged that God was the owner of all, then he blessed Abraham. The priest brought forth bread and wine. This represented the blood and body of Jesus, the act of communion.

I Corinthians 15:23 calls Jesus Christ the firstfruits, and the Bible calls the tithes the firstfruits. Melchizedek was ministering God's firstfruits, which is Christ, to Abraham. Abraham ministered back to the priest his firstfruits, which is tithes. Abraham was demonstrating that he was a believer and that God was Lord of his life.

Many Christians say that Christ is Lord of their life, but walk around with filthy lucre or unrighteous mammon--money that has not been tithed on--in their pocket or stacked in their bank. It remains filthy until it is tithed on. The tithe unto the Lord changes your money into blessed money. That is how 90% goes further than 100%. Romans 11:16 says, "For if the firstfruit be holy, the lump is also holy: and if the root be holy, so are the branches."

The principle of firstfruits is an integral part of our heritage. It deals not only with money, but it deals with our salvation. When the priests would receive the sheaf of grain, they would wave it up and down and across from side to side. They were waving it in the form of a cross. Jesus was the wave offering for us and as He suffered on that cross, was buried, and then resurrected from the cold tomb, He became the firstfruits of the resurrection. Jesus was made holy and acceptable; therefore, because the firstfruits was made holy, we are made holy and acceptable unto God when we give ourselves to Him. He is the root, we are the branches.

We demonstrate this principle every time we bring our tithe unto the Lord. We are saying, "Jesus is Lord of my life, and I bring my firstfruit to Him, in acknowledgment to Him that He became my firstfruit." In Biblical times, the first act of harvest worships the harvest's Lord. The first sickle cuts an offering for God. Thought of God should precede all. Let morning dawn with Him. Let Him always be first in our thoughts in everything we do.

One speaker I listened to on tithing made the observation that the priests put hoops in the field at the time of planting, and then when it was harvest, two priests would go to the field and cut the grain before the people could start the harvesting for themselves.

The more I thought upon it, the more it bothered me. Why would the priests have to go to the field and get it when the people were instructed to bring it willingly to the Lord? After study and research, I found that the tithing system had fallen into disarray and the people had grown careless with their giving. When Nehemiah was rebuilding the walls and bringing restoration to the proper order of God's system, he appointed the priest to gather the tithes. This was because of a breakdown of the original plan.

The scripture gives us this account at the time of temple order was being restored:

And at that time were some appointed over the chambers for the treasures, for the offerings, for the firstfruits, and for the tithes, to gather into them out of the fields of the cities the portions of the law for the priests and Levites... (Nehemiah 12:44).

It is much more blessed to give than to have someone come and get it from you. When the order of giving the firstfruits was first instituted, it was brought willingly unto the priest. Abraham gave willingly. Jacob gave willingly even when he had nothing. He made a promise on those rocks that memorial day that everything God blessed him with, he would give God a tenth (Genesis 28:22). Jacob became a very rich man because of this practice. Those that bring willingly are always blessed.

Notice another interesting thing that happened in the Bible, this one under Hezekiah's reign. Israel had degenerated into idol worship, and along with that decline the tithing system also was forgotten. Hezekiah brought reform and revival back to the people. First, he destroyed the idols. Secondly, he restored the burnt-offerings and organized the priests to give thanks, and to praise the Lord. Thirdly, he commanded the people that dwelt in Jerusalem to give the portion of the priests to them.

And as soon as the commandment came abroad, the children of Israel brought in abundance the firstfruits of corn, wine, and oil, and honey, and of all the increase of the field; and *the tithe of all things brought they in abundantly* (II Chronicles 31:5).

When a person's heart is made right he gives abundantly. When his heart has wedges of bitterness, discontent, and disillusionment in it, he withholds from God and the ministry of the church. He forgets that God is the receiver of the tithes. He gets his eyes on man, and forgets the whole purpose and order of tithing. He is not displeasing man when he does not tithe; he is displeasing God.

The concept of firstfruits is from Genesis to Revelation, and is closely connected with the plan of salvation. Jesus Christ became the firstfruits for mankind and ministers to us. We give the firstfruits of ourselves, our possessions, our increase, our everything, and minister back to God. It is not an optional thing. It is a commandment. If a person disobeys a commandment of God he does not receive the blessing--he receives the opposite, which is a curse.

In Deuteronomy 26, after the people had brought their firstfruits to the Lord, He pronounced a blessing upon them.

> Thou hast avouched the Lord this day to be thy God, and to walk in his ways, and to keep his statutes, and his commandments, and his judgments, and to hearken unto his voice: And the Lord hath avouched thee this day to be his peculiar people, as he hath promised thee, and that thou shouldest keep all his commandments; And to make thee high above all nations which he hath made, in praise, and in name, and in honour; and that thou mayest be an holy people unto the Lord thy God, as he hath spoken (Deuteronomy 26:17-19).

You say, "That was the children of Israel, Abraham's seed." Yes, but we have the same blessings because of the Lord Jesus Christ.

> Christ hath redeemed us from the curse of the law, being made a curse for us: for it is written, Cursed is every one that hangeth on a tree: That the blessing of Abraham might come on the Gentiles through Jesus Christ; that we might receive the promise of the Spirit through faith. And if ye be Christ's, then are ye

Abraham's seed, and heirs according to the promise (Galatians 3:13-14, 29).

Do not seek to understand how the blessing works, but it works because God said it. There was once a man from Baalshalisha that came to Elisha and brought him bread of the firstfruits, twenty loaves of barley, and full ears of corn. He told him to give it unto the people that they may eat. Elisha said, "What, should I set this before an hundred men? He said again, Give the people, that they may eat: for thus saith the Lord, They shall eat" (II Kings 4:43). When Elisha set the tithe of the land before the hundred men, they ate and left full. God always makes up any difference. There is no lack with Him.

Remember this: "And all the tithe of the land, whether of the seed of the land, or of the fruit of the tree, is the LORD'S: it is holy unto the Lord" (Leviticus 27:30). The tithe is holy or precious unto the Lord. Who are we to make it unholy?

Remember this also:

Woe unto you, scribes and Pharisees, hypocrites! for ye pay tithe of mint and anise and cummin, and have omitted the weightier matters of the law, judgment, mercy, and faith: these ought ye to have done, and *not to leave the other undone* (Matthew 23:23).

This was a backhanded compliment. It was the only time Jesus came close to commending the Pharisees, but He did tell them, "You are doing something right, but not everything." Jesus did not tell them, "You do not have to pay your tithes anymore." No, He told them they should pay their tithes.

When you understand the principle of giving, you will be excited to give, for firstfruits is closely interwoven with Calvary, showing that Christ was our firstfruit. As we approach His throne, let us bring our tithe, offerings, and selves generously to Him, the Master. Let us say, "Father, I thank you for what you have already given me, and I am sowing to the future. You are my source, and I depend solely upon you. Here is my gift, my best, my portion, and my all."

Let these scriptures be food for thought for you on the word *first:*

Honour the Lord with *firstfruits* (Proverbs 3:9).

Seek ye *first* the kingdom of God (Matthew 6:33).

And Jesus answered him, The *first* of all the commandments is, Hear, O Israel; The Lord our God is one Lord: And thou shalt love the Lord thy God with *all thy heart, and with all thy soul, and with all thy mind, and with all thy strength:* this is the *first* commandment (Mark 12:29-30).

...Ourselves also, which have the *firstfruits* of the Spirit... (Romans 8:23--Jesus was our firstfruit, and He gave us His spirit.)

And this they did, not as we hoped, but *first* gave their own selves to the Lord... (II Corinthians 8:5).

Chapter 4

ARE OFFERINGS NECESSARY?

Offerings are something you offer unto God. They are to be presented as an act of worship or sacrifice. *Of* means from, indicating derivation, separation, source; belonging to or separated from, to give of one's energy. *Off* means so as to be no longer supported, attached or united; as, to take off the hat. Thus the root words *of* and *off* indicate a separation or giving away. An offering is something that you offer or give away. It belongs to you, but you make it available to someone else. To offer is to make the first advance, to present or bring. Paying tithes is not enough. Offerings must also be included to receive the blessing of the Lord.

Someone has said, "Tithes opens the windows, and offerings determines how much is poured down." Again, let us quote Malachi 3:8. "Will a man rob God? Yet ye have robbed me. But ye say, Wherein have we robbed thee? In tithes and offerings." There is a difference between them. Tithes is God's already, and the initial amount is determined for you. The guesswork is taken out of it, whereas offerings are open to your discretion.

Wouldn't it be wonderful to have people with such a willing spirit of giving that the offerings they brought were more than enough? Two examples of offerings that were more than enough are found in I Chronicles and Exodus.

In the first, David spoke to all the people about the building of the house of God:

> Now I have prepared with all my might for the house of my God the gold for things to be made of gold, and the silver for things of silver, and the brass for things of brass, the iron for things of iron, and wood for things of wood; onyx stones, and stones to be set, glistening stones, and of divers colours, and all manner of precious stones, and marble stones in abundance. Moreover, because I have set my affection to the house of my God, I have of *mine own* proper good, of gold and silver, which *I have given* to the house of my God, *over and above* all that I have prepared for the holy house...who then is willing to consecrate his service this day unto the Lord?...Then the people rejoiced, for that they offered willingly, because with perfect heart they offered willingly to the Lord; and David the king also rejoiced with great joy (I Chronicles 29:2-3,5b,9).

Notice the end of David's life. "And he died in a good old age, full of days, riches, and honour..." (I Chronicles 29:28). One characteristic of David was that he always did everything with zeal and a willing heart. He may have sinned, but even in his sin, he willingly and quickly repented and asked for forgiveness. Even in his giving, he gave over and above. He always gave more than was required. He gave and God prospered him abundantly.

The other incident occurred when Moses gathered all the children of Israel together and told them about the plan for the building of the tabernacle. "...The Lord commanded saying, Take ye from among you an offering unto the Lord: whosoever is of a willing heart, let him bring it, an offering of the Lord; gold, and silver, and brass" (Exodus 35:4b-5).

Notice their response. "The children of Israel brought a willing offering unto the Lord, every man and woman" (Exodus 35:29a). Then the leaders in charge of the offering told Moses,

> The people bring much more than enough for the service of the work, which the Lord commanded to make. And Moses gave commandment, and they caused it to be proclaimed throughout the camp, saying, Let neither man nor woman make any more work for the offering of the sanctuary. So the people were restrained from bringing. For the stuff they had was sufficient for all the work to make it, and too much (Exodus 36:5-7).

This amazes me! They actually had to tell the people to quit bringing their offerings because the total given was already too much. It would be a wonderful problem for the church today if the preacher could say, "Do not give any more. We have sufficient over and above what we need."

Notice that both the above offerings were given willingly. That is what an offering is. It is giving our best willingly, cheerfully and excitedly.

In the account of Cain and Abel, there is a key word that indicates why God did not accept Cain's offering.

...Abel was a keeper of sheep, but Cain was a tiller of the ground. And in process of time it came to pass, that Cain brought of the fruit of the ground an offering unto the Lord. And Abel, he also brought of the firstlings of his flock and of the fat thereof. And the Lord had respect unto Abel and to his offering: But unto Cain and to his offering he had not respect (Genesis 4:2b-5a).

The key word is firstlings. Abel brought what was equivalent to the firstfruits, which was required by God. Cain seemingly just brought fruit, but not the firstfruits. Cain's attitude was not right; if he would have had a right spirit he would not have killed his brother. He was eaten up with jealousy, envy, and pride, and was only going through the motions of doing what he was taught to do. He did not bring his best. He did not advertise this fact, but God looks not only at the offering, He looks first at the heart or the attitude of the giver.

There is a golden thread that weaves itself from Genesis to Revelation and that is the fact that God will only accept our best. He will not take second-best. He required the firstfruits, and He requires all the heart. The Lord spoke to Moses and told him to speak unto Aaron, his sons, and all the children of Israel about the offerings to be made to Him. He said,

> But whatsoever hath a blemish, that shall ye not offer: for it shall not be acceptable for you. And whosoever offereth a sacrifice of peace-offerings unto the Lord to accomplish his vow, or a freewill offering in beeves or sheep, it shall be perfect to be accepted; there shall be no blemish therein. Blind, or broken, or maimed, or having a wen, or scurvy, or scabbed, ye shall not offer these unto the Lord, nor make an offering by fire of them upon the altar unto the Lord. Ye shall not offer unto the Lord that which is bruised, or crushed, or broken, or cut (Leviticus 22:20-22,24).

The Lord spoke to Israel by Malachi and He told them He loved Jacob, but hated Esau. He rebuked the priests telling them they had despised His name. When they asked how they had despised His name, He answered,

> ...Ye offer the blind for sacrifice, is it not evil? and if ye offer the lame and sick, is it not evil?...For from the rising of the sun even unto the going down of the same my name shall be great among the Gentiles; and in every place incense shall be offered unto my name, and a pure offering: for my name shall be great among the heathen, saith the Lord of hosts. But ye have

profaned it, in that ye say, The table of the Lord is polluted; and the fruit thereof, even his meat, is contemptible. Ye said also, Behold what a weariness is it! and ye have snuffed at it, said the Lord of hosts; and ye brought that which was torn, and the lame, and the sick; thus ye brought an offering: should I accept this of your hand? saith the Lord (Malachi 1:8,11-13).

Could it be the reason there is so much trouble among Christians is not only because of Satan's doings, but because we have offered less than our best in our offerings, service, attitudes, and commitment? Are we sighing with the words, "It is such a heavy load. It is a weariness to do what He has asked me to do." Are our hearts on fire with zeal and love, or are we only going through the motions offering to God our leftovers? Has the modern-day church gone wild with buying up the goods of this world so much that they can barely pay their tithes, and are sometimes late on that because of their commitment to the creditors? Do things bid for our money to the point so that we can only give a dollar in the offering?

We think nothing of plunking down a $10.00 bill for a dinner, but hesitate to give "that much" in an offering. Our priorities are sick. We are measuring things on the scale of sight and tangibles, instead of eternity and the unseen. We will pay $100.00 for a dress or a suit of clothes that we really do not need, but to give $100.00 to a regular offering, why, we would faint on the floor before we were able to do that! Oh, the money that goes down the drain every day is preposterous.

I utter a warning to this generation to wake up! We are being tempted to offer God less than our best and are giving our best for the things which money can buy. You say, "Oh, I give God my best." Examine your monthly budget and see where your money goes, and then see if He is first on your list. Examine your thoughts and attitudes in giving to God.

Offerings were as much a part of God's initial plan as were the tithes. There was the:

Trespass Offering	Leviticus 5:15,19
Meat Offering	Leviticus 2:1-3,11
Burnt Offering	Exodus 29:10-18
Heave Offering	Exodus 29:28
Drink Offering	Genesis 35:14
Sin Offering	Exodus 29:14
Wave Offering	Exodus 29:24

He said in Deuteronomy 16:10, "And thou shalt keep the feast of weeks unto the Lord thy God with a tribute of a freewill-offering of thine hand, which thou shalt give unto the Lord thy God, according as the Lord thy God hath blessed thee." This is in accordance with the incident of the widow that gave her all, whereas the rich men only gave out of their abundance. Jesus said to give according to how you are blessed. A $10.00 bill would be a lot for some, but for others it would be like a penny. So for two people to give the same amount would not be the same to the Lord; He judges what you have left and how much more you could have given.

I urge you not to just haphazardly give to the Lord. Make it an important thing. From personal experience, I know it works. One of the most recent things that has happened to me occurred this year. The Lord impressed me to increase by ten times the amount I was giving in each church service offering. Since that time, God has been pouring blessings on me. Just last night, He impressed me to up it another five percent. It is the most exciting thing. I have discovered that God's plan really works, and I cannot wait to give it. He has taught me to live totally by faith.

Last week, a man who was doing some work for us told me he needed a certain amount of money by the next day. I had thought we had more time to get the money together. So I told God, "You are my supplier, and I am depending on you. You said, 'Prove me,' so I know you will have the money there at the appointed time." My husband was out of the country at the time, so he could not help me get the funds together.

Imagine my ecstasy when I went to the mailbox and found two checks that covered what we needed, plus a little more. One check we were expecting. The other one was totally unexpected, but God knew the exact time to have it in the mailbox. You cannot improve on God's system. It works. A hundred times over I say it works! He said, "Prove me now." You do it His way with the right attitude, and it is guaranteed--backed by all of the authority of heaven.

Chapter 5

REWARD OF MONETARY GIVING

Your financial condition will be determined by your obedience in giving and the attitude wherewith you give. Philippians 4:19 says God shall supply all your needs, but this promise does not start there. It begins with verse 15, where Paul speaks to the Philippians who were the only missions givers among the early churches. Because of their regular support, he spoke this blessing upon them.

The wealthy Baron de Rothschild once posed before an artist as a beggar. While the artist, Ary Scheffer, was painting him, the financier sat before him in rags and tatters holding a tin cup. The artist's friend entered, and the baron was so perfectly disguised that he was not recognized. The visitor, thinking he was really a beggar, gave him a coin. The pretended model put the coin in his pocket. Ten years later the man who gave it to him received a letter from de Rothschild containing a bank order for 10,000 francs and the following message:

"You one day gave a coin to Baron de Rothschild in the studio of Ary Scheffer. He has invested it and today sends you the capital which you entrusted to him, together with the compounded interest. A good action always brings good fortune." The note was signed "Baron de Rothschild."

On receipt of the order the surprised contributor sought out the baron, a billionaire, who proved to him from the account books that under his management this small amount had swelled to this large sum.

Christ is walking through the world unrecognized today. Blessed are those who give to Him in the person of His poor brethren or take the Gospel to those who have it not. Blessed are they who give their money and service to the kingdom of heaven; it pays rich dividends.

Jesus over and over scorned the man who did nothing with his money or talent, but just buried it. He emphasized the fact that you have to invest to increase. For example, at the rate of a dollar a day it would take 2,740 years to save $1,000,000; the same dollar invested daily at eight percent interest, compounded semiannually, will reach the million mark in 66 years.

Benjamin Franklin left a fund of $5,000 to the city of Boston in 1791. His will provided that interest from this fund be allowed to accumulate for 300 years. By 1891, the $5,000 had grown to $92,000, and the balance was invested for a second century. By 1959, the market value of the Boston trust fund was $1.5 million, and the Massachusetts Supreme Judicial Court has reaffirmed that the fund should continue. Apparently Benjamin Franklin knew what he was talking about when he said, "Money begets money and its offspring begets more."

Epictetus said, "No great thing is created suddenly, any more than a bunch of grapes or a fig. If you tell me that you desire a fig, I answer you that there must be time. Let it first blossom, then bear fruit, then ripen."

The late Spencer Penrose, brother of Philadelphia political leader Boies Penrose, was regarded by his family as a black sheep for choosing to live in the West instead of the East. Penrose went to Colorado Springs in 1891 fresh out of Harvard. He had not been there long before he wired his brother for $1500 to go into a mining deal. His brother telegraphed him $150 for train fare and warned him to come home.

Years later Spencer returned to Philadelphia and handed Boies $75,000 in gold coin. Boies looked amazed, then reminded Spencer that he had not gone into the deal and had sent him only $150. "That," replied Spencer, "is why I'm giving you only $75,000. If you'd sent me the $1500, I would be giving you three-quarters of a million."

Can you imagine what would happen if the church started being as careful with their investments to God? How much more of a yield would there be? Ron Knott, the Delta airline pilot, gave his testimony at our church in June 1992. It was so inspirational and biblically-based, and showed how God works when a person operates totally according to His plan. It is a prime example what happens when God is first and foremost in our finances.

He said, "My money can work for me 24 hours a day. I've never lost one dollar. I've invested in the economy of God. One of the greatest things we can do is invest in God's economy, and God will use it to reach people all over the world. You can't outgive God. Will God repay you? I would rather be blessed with the windows of heaven than with the windows of Las Vegas, some crooked business deal, or the lottery. With God's riches you get peace and joy in the Holy Ghost.

"A friend of mine called me from Louisiana and told me about an oil and gas company fixing to sell out. It had four oil wells on 640 acres of land. He said there was surface equipment that had been sitting around and there had been no production for fifteen 15 years. There was a little bit of residual gas in the ground because they used it for a storage area at one time. Somebody would make a little bit off of it.

"We prayed about it and then bid on it. Neither one of us had any money, but we were the highest bidder. We had to go to the bank and convince them we knew what we were doing, but we really didn't.

"We decided to give the first $25,000 to God. We would probably close it down in about six weeks at the most. We did not do anything but go out and turn four rusty valves on that had not produced in fifteen years, and the gas started flowing. The first month that we got our check, it was for $25,000. Eleven years later it was still pumping gas and we had taken over two million dollars out of the ground. We sold the property a year ago to a large oil company out of Shreveport, and it hasn't produced a thing since. You tell me God wasn't in that. You tell me that God will not reward you for what you give to Him."

At the end of Chapter 7 you will find the Deuteronomy 26 attitude Bro. Mahaney brought to light, which I referred to in the Acknowledgments. He told me last night, which was a Monday, that his wife had called him with exciting news. He said that he and his wife had done the Deuteronomy 26 approach for the first time this last month, and that after service a man came up to him and handed him $500.00. He also said that the IRS had written to them and told them they owed the government money, and that after checking certain papers they would let them know how much. The Mahaneys were expecting any day the letter telling them the amount they owed. Monday the letter came, and instead of them owing the IRS, the IRS sent them several hundred dollars back. He said, "It works!"

God cannot lie. He said according to what you give is what you will receive back. If we give abundantly, we will receive abundantly. If we give modestly, we will receive modestly. Job said, "For he maketh small the drops of water: they pour down rain according to the vapour thereof" (Job 36:27). Whatever is sent up and invested in God's economy will return. Someone has said, "You can't take your money with you, but you can send it on ahead."

Chapter 6

GREED AND MONEY

Greed is an acquisitive desire beyond reason; to crave selfishly in excess. It includes cupidity which is an inordinate desire, especially for wealth; avarice, or lust. *Avarice* is excessive or inordinate desire of gain; greediness after wealth, and covetousness. *Inordinate* is lacking order or right arrangement, disorderly, or unrestrained; not limited to rules prescribed, nor to the usual boundary; excessive and immoderate.

Horace Greeley wrote, "The darkest hour in any man's life is when he sits down to plan how to get money without earning it."

In Tolstoy's *Man and Dame*, Fortune the hero is told he can have the right to all of the land around which he can plow a furrow in a single day. The man started off with great vigor, and was going to encompass only that which he could easily care for. But as the day progressed he desired more and more. He plowed and plowed, until at the end of the day he could in no possible way return to his original point of departure, but struggling to do so, he fell, the victim of a heart attack.

Greece was the most highly cultured nation of her time. Rome reached a zenith of tremendous power. Both went down in a crash of selfishness, indulgence and immorality. Greed and lust were the foundations of these two great governments, and they fell because of them. When self reigns, it always brings a fall.

Greed usually has money attached to it. When Mordecai would not bow down and reverence Haman, the newly appointed prince in Ahasuerus' kingdom, Haman became enraged. He determined that Mordecai and all his people, the Jews, would die. He plotted, schemed, and had gallows built to kill and mortify Mordecai. Haman wanted to make an example of Mordecai to all the people that they must honor his leadership and position.

As usual, his diabolical plot had money connected with it. When Mordecai heard the news, he and his people started praying and fasting to God for deliverance. Then Esther sent Hatach, one of the king's chamberlains whom he had appointed to attend her, and gave him a commandment to go and talk with Mordecai about it. When Hatach reached Mordecai, the truth came out.

"And Mordecai told him of all that had happened unto him, and of the sum of the money that Haman had promised to pay to the king's treasuries for the Jews, to destroy them" (Esther 4:7). Haman's greed for power was accompanied by a very lucrative promise. Money talked to the king, but after the Jews talked to God through prayer and fasting, God changed it all around. God had more power than the money. Greed got Haman the noose around his own neck. This is what always happens to those who are driven by greed and selfishness.

The bottom line of greed is self. Self wants power. Self wants prestige and honor. The root word of selfishness, which means exclusive regard to one's own interest, is self. Usually greed is so strong an emotion in the mind and heart of the one it possesses that it makes the person take advantage of others while attaining what he wants.

When King Ahab wanted the vineyard of Naboth, he was willing to do anything to get it. The king was obsessed with greed, whereas Naboth was filled with honor. Many people could be bought with money, but not Naboth.

The following scripture gives a clue to his character: "...I spake unto Naboth the Jezreelite, and said unto him, Give me thy vineyard for money;...and he answered, I will not give thee my vineyard" (I Kings 21:6). It was a vineyard handed down from generation to generation. He was told never to sell it, but to care for it and hand it down to his sons and their sons. The honor of a family plan meant more to him than the king's money.

The Psalm says, "Trust not in oppression, and become not vain in robbery: if riches increase, set not your heart upon them" (Psalm 62:10). Greed trusts in and desires riches, and will do almost anything to get them, even cheat a little.

Paul warns Titus about the love of money: "For a bishop must be blameless, as the steward of God; not self-willed, not soon angry, not given to wine, no striker, not given to filthy lucre" (Titus 1:7). *Lucre* means gain in money, profit or riches in a bad sense. Thus this verse in Titus means to not be greedy of base gain or dishonest gain. It also means not to give yourself to just making money, but to give yourselves to the things of the spirit. "Till I come, give attendance to reading, to exhortation, to doctrine" (I Timothy 4:13).

The example of the apostles shows that they gave themselves to prayer and the word. "But we will give ourselves continually to prayer, and to the ministry of the word" (Acts 6:4). Can you imagine what would happen if all the leadership would do this? Revival would be great among us!

Money has been here since the beginning of time and is first referred to in Genesis 17:27. It is referred to as being an answer to all things (Ecclesiastes 10:19), but also it has been stated that the love of money is the root of all evil.

"For the love of money is the root of all evil; which while some coveted after, they have erred from the faith, and pierced themselves through with many sorrows. But thou O man of God, flee these things" (I Timothy 6:10-11a). What things? A covetousness and love for money. Jesus said it this way: "But seek ye first the kingdom of God, and his righteousness; and all these things shall be added unto you" (Matthew 6:33). What things? Food, clothing, and the things that money can buy.

I promise you that if you will seek after the things of God and follow God's tithing and offering plan, you will have more than enough. God and man will shower blessings unto you abundantly. That doesn't mean you just sit back and not work. No, you work, but your work is not your god. It is your response to the commandment of God. Man is commanded to work, but not to be a slave to it. Good stewardship and right priorities all enter into the plan of God. "Wealth gotten by vanity shall be diminished: but he that gathereth by labour shall increase" (Proverbs 13:11). *Vanity* here means idleness and falseness.

Increase is promised when you obey the commandments of God.

Now these are the commandments, the statutes, and the judgments, which the Lord your God commanded to teach you...that thou mightest fear the Lord thy God, to keep all his statutes and his commandments...that it may be well with thee, and that ye may increase mightily, as the Lord God of thy fathers hath promised thee... (Deuteronomy 6:1-3).

Learn to be a good steward over your time, mind, money, character and all things that the Lord has given you. It is a proven fact that if you cannot budget a small amount you surely cannot budget a larger amount. Now is the time to get control of your finances and not wait until that magical day in the future when buckets of money are poured into your lap. As you show God you are faithful over the little amount and give Him His proper share, you will be increased, but do not wait to get more money to start giving to God. It will never be right until you put some reins on your spending and live on the income you now have. For some people there is never enough money no matter how much money they make.

A story told by Dale Carnegie bears this out. Mrs. Elsie Stapleton, a woman who spent years as financial advisor to the customers both of Wanamaker's Department Store in New York and of Gimbel's, spent additional years as an individual consultant. She helped people with incomes of $1000 a year to $100,000 a year. She said, "More money is not the answer to most people's financial worries. In fact, I have often seen it happen that an increase in income accomplished nothing but an increase in spending--and an increase in headaches."

"What causes most people to worry," she said, "is not that they haven't enough money, but that they don't know how to spend the money they have." It is important to have a plan for spending your money and spend accordingly. Know where every nickel you spend has gone. Keep a record--have a budget.

Once when Paul Getty was interviewed the question was asked, "If you retired now, would you say your holdings would be worth a billion dollars?"

Getty paced up and down the room and then answered the question, "I suppose so, but remember a billion doesn't go as far as it used to."

Benjamin Franklin said, "Money never made a man happy yet, nor will it. There is nothing in its nature to produce happiness. The more a man has, the more he wants. Instead of its filling a vacuum, it makes one. If it satisfies one want, it doubles and trebles that want another way. That was a true proverb of the wise man; rely upon it: 'Better is little with the fear of the Lord, than great treasure, and trouble therewith.' "

Just remember that in getting money, you are only receiving something cold and dead. "For wisdom is a defence, and money is a defence: but the excellency of knowledge is, that wisdom giveth life to them that have it" (Ecclesiastes 7:12). Wisdom giveth life, but money does not. Money is only a medium of exchange, and what you do with it determines your destiny. It is important what you do with your money. The more you give to the bank of heaven, the more you will have that will not burn up in the end. The interest heaven pays is far superior to the interest earth offers.

The story of Rockefeller intrigues me. He became so wealthy that he worried night and day about his money. He became a hated man by many because he was so obsessed with greed, drive, and ambition to get more money. At age 53, he became deathly sick and was forced to do something about it. The doctors said he would have to retire. Before he retired, worry, greed, and fear had already wrecked his health. He retired, but he did something else that changed his life. He started reflecting and thinking of other people. Instead of thinking how much money he could get, he began to wonder how much that money would buy in terms of human happiness. He started giving his millions away. He learned of a starving little college on the shores of Lake Michigan that was being foreclosed because of its mortgage. He came to its rescue and poured millions of dollars into that college and built it into the world-famous University of Chicago.

He established the Rockefeller Foundation which was to fight disease and ignorance all over the world. Research was undertaken; colleges were founded; doctors worked to find the causes of disease and it was all paid for by Rockefeller's millions.

What happened to Rockefeller when he started helping other people? There was such a drastic change in him that it startled his friends. He no longer worried, but was happy and relaxed. The man who was to die at age 53 lived to be 98 years old.

Jesus gave the formula for true life. He said,

Lay not up for yourselves treasures upon earth, where moth and rust doth corrupt, and where thieves break through and steal: But lay up for yourselves treasures in heaven, where neither moth nor rust doth corrupt, and where thieves do not break through nor steal: For where your treasure is, there will your heart be also (Matthew 6:19-21).

Greed for money can numb your brain and crowd out more important things. There is an impressive story told about the search for gold in the Klondike. A prospecting party, penetrating far into the country, came upon a miner's hut. All without was as quiet as the grave.

Entering the cabin, they found the skeletons of two men and a large quantity of gold. On a rough table was a letter telling of their successful search for the precious ore. In their eagerness to get it, they forgot the early coming of winter in that northern land.

One morning they awoke to find a great snowstorm upon them. For days the tempest raged, cutting off all hope of escape. Their little store of food was soon gone, and they lay down and died amidst abounding gold. Their folly was not in finding the gold, but in neglecting to provide against the winter.

Tell me how you spend your money and I'll tell you where your heart is. The question for all of us to ponder is, "Where is my heart?" or "Who has my heart--God or greed?"

The story is told about the sailor who stopped at a small inn at a village in Normandie. He engaged supper and a night's lodging. The landlord and his wife were old and appeared to be poor. The sailor asked them to eat with him and during the meal he inquired about the family, asking especially about a son who went to sea when a lad. They supposed he was dead, as nothing had been heard from him for years.

At bedtime the landlady showed the sailor to his room. He bade her "Good night," then slipped a little purse of gold into her hand. She showed the purse to her husband and the two were delighted at the sight of it. They surmised that the sailor must have more in his possession. During the night they murdered him in bed and took all his money.

Early the next morning two of the lodger's relatives came to inquire about him. They said he had left. "That isn't possible," they said, "for he was your son and he had come home to spend his life with you. He told us he would stay with you one night and see how kind you might be to

59

a stranger." They had murdered their own son because of the cursed love of gold.

How many today are ready to sell their souls to the devil for a purse of gold! How many families are sacrificed on the altar of the almighty dollar? Does greed have a small place in your heart? What motivates you? Examine your heart and lay everything on the altar that would hinder you from taking you, your family, and others to the place where gold will be walked upon. Gold will not be God there; it will only be something under our feet. Now is the time to put its influence under our feet and use it to provide for our families and churches, and to lay up treasures in heaven. Who is the boss--you or your money? You should control it, not it control you!

> No man can serve two masters: for either he will hate the one, and love the other, or else he will hold to the one, and despise the other. Ye cannot serve God and mammon (Matthew 6:24).

Mammon is riches. Used as a proper name by Milton the poet, it represents the demon of cupidity, one of the fallen angels. As I have already stated, cupidity means to long for, desire, or covet.

Although a Christian should be a good steward over what God has given him, he should not lust after becoming rich. He should hunger after the things of God, and when he is blessed by God, he should give abundantly to further the cause of Christ on earth.

When the rich young ruler was told by Jesus to sell all he had and feed the poor, he turned sorrowfully away, because his riches had him; he did not have the power over the riches. The ironic thing is that if he would have given it all away, Jesus would have given more back to him. The Word says, "he that lendeth to the poor, lendeth unto the Lord" (Proverbs 19:17).

How much can God entrust unto you? Will you give it back into His hands, or will you hoard it up while a world passes by you hungry, destitute, lost without hope? The blessings of the Lord given unto you are to be shared with God and others. God's economy is based on giving. You give away--God gives it back! Who will your master be-- God or money? You can be poor, and money can be your master, for it does not master only the rich.

What compels you? What excites you the most when it comes to money? What is more important, helping some- one who has less than you, or buying something new for yourself?

As Milton made mammon one of the fallen angels, I say, let us cast it away from us! Let us desire to please the God of the universe and follow His master plan. Let us not bow down and worship at the feet of mammon in our hearts, but as we are blessed, let us bless others and the cause of God!

One last question: Are you giving unto God out of your abundance, or out of your want as the little widow woman gave when Jesus commended her? And if you are giving out of your want, is it because you have been a bad steward over your money, or spent it on so many things that you have nothing left to give to God? Let us be honest as we examine our heart and pocketbook. Ask forgiveness, begin anew, and determine to do it God's way from this day forward. Today is the first day of the rest of your life, and the way things are, the rest of your life could be short if the rapture takes place soon. This is the day to stop short-changing God, to quit kidding yourself, and to set your house in order and walk in awe before the Lord.

Chapter 7

ATTITUDE OF THE GIVER

But this I say, He which soweth sparingly shall reap also sparingly; and he which soweth bountifully shall reap also bountifully. Every man according as he purposeth in his heart, so let him give; nor grudgingly, or of necessity: for God loveth a cheerful giver (II Corinthians 9:6-7). Although this principle of giving can be applied to all things, Paul is actually talking about monetary giving. In the first verse he talks about ministering to the saints; in verse 12 he refers to supplying the wants of the saints; in verse 13 he talks about their liberal distribution unto them. God loves the giver that gives cheerfully.

This is the only scripture in the entire Bible that uses the particular phrase "God loves." If God loves something, I want to understand what it is He loves. The scripture says that God loves the *person* that gives, not the money given. His plan is for the money to come through His people, but His object of affection is not what is brought, but the bearer of the gift. Notice three things about verses 6 and 7: God does not want a person to give grudgingly, or of necessity, but cheerfully.

Let us examine the three words in the order they are given. We need to know what they mean, for we ought to get as far away as possible from the first two, and run towards the third.

GRUDGINGLY: The verb *grudge* means to be loath to give, or to give with reluctance, or with desire to get back again; to covet, to envy the possession of; to murmur, grumble, grouse, or grouch about it. The noun *grudge* means complaint, grumbling, reluctance, uneasiness of conscience, sullen malice or cherished ill will.

NECESSITY: That which is necessary; that which is unavoidable because compelled; the negation of freedom in voluntary action--contrasted with freedom or liberty.

CHEERFUL: Full of cheer; having, or showing good spirits; cheering; contented, enlivening; also, without grudging or grumbling; hearty. What is cheer? *Cheer* means to urge on or encourage by word or deed, especially by shouts, cries, or cheers; to salute or applaud with cheers, or shouts of approval; to become gladsome or joyous, rejoice; make merry; to utter a shout or shouts of applause, triumph. A *cheerer* is one who cheers, applauds, or hurrahs. *Cheerfulness* is gladness, merriment, gaiety, mirth, hilarity, glee. Cheerfulness implies a bright and equable temper or disposition, which shows itself in the face, the voice, the actions; it suggests a strong and spontaneous flow of good spirits. Mirth is short and transient, whereas cheerfulness is fixed and permanent.

Cheerfulness keeps up a kind of daylight in the mind, and fills it with serenity.

There it is. When you murmur or grumble about giving your tithes and offerings to God, you displease God. What He does with that displeasure towards you is up to Him, but He has a track record of withholding blessing from those that murmur against His plan.

Notice what he did in Numbers 11.

And when the people complained, it displeased the Lord: and the Lord heard it; and his anger was kindled; and the fire of the Lord burnt among them, and consumed them that were in the uttermost parts of the camp. And the people cried unto Moses; and when Moses prayed unto the Lord, the fire was quenched (Numbers 11:1-2).

If grouching or giving reluctantly displeases the Lord, we need to repent if we have been guilty of that attitude. Also, if we give just because we are asked to give and feel responsible to give just because of the need, we are sinning. We are not to say, "Well, if I have to give, I guess I'll give. If I don't give who else will give?" God forbid that any Christian would grumble about giving or give only because he feels compelled to give.

If you want God's love and approval it is time to change your attitude about giving. God loves the one who feels good about giving, who can't wait to give, and is so excited about it that it shows in his face and posture. How long has it been since you rejoiced all the way to the offering plate? How long has it been since you were so eager to give you could hardly wait for the pastor to take the offering?

What do you say to your family on the way to church? Do you say, "I am so excited! I cannot wait to get to church so I can give my tithes and offering unto the Lord!" Or do you say, "I wonder what offering or need the pastor will dream up tonight for us to feel guilty about if we do not give to it?" Do you spread a feeling among your family that the money you make is yours and you barely eke out enough to soothe your conscience to give to God? Is it a painful experience for you to let go of your money? If it is, you need a spiritual heart surgery. Walk, better yet, run to the altar and ask God to forgive you for your greed, covetousness, and selfishness. Ask Him to give you a spirit of giving so you can give cheerfully unto the Lord.

The closest thing to most people's heart is their money, but the thing is, the money is only loaned to them from God. "And thou say in thine heart, My power and the might of mine hand hath gotten me this wealth. But thou shalt remember the Lord thy God: for it is he that giveth thee power to get wealth..." (Deuteronomy 8:17-18). It is not your money. Nothing is yours. It is only a gift or loan from God for a season of time. You are only a steward of all He gives to you. He gave you a mind, He gives you time, He gives you strength, a heart, and a will. He has given each person many things. Each individual must answer to God for what he did with each gift that was given to him by Almighty God. We cannot squander, misuse, or lazily let rot the things He has given us; we must be diligent about our Father's business.

Someone once said, "People should consider that they are only trustees for what they possess, and should show their wealth to be more in doing good than merely in having it." Let this concept burn in your brain: "I am a trustee or a steward for a season of time over everything that I possess or that has been given to me. What I do with it determines my destiny."

John Wesley always said, "When I have any money, I get rid of it as quickly as possible, lest it find a way into my heart." What is in your heart? A love for God or a desire for more money? What would get you out of bed at night--a business deal with promise of more money or an urgency to pray? What excites you the most? Making money or giving money to the many needs of the spreading of the gospel? Do you let the Word of God control your giving or are you influenced in a negative way because a few men of God have failed in their stewardship and have bilked the people? Where is your confidence? You are not giving to the man, you are giving to God. God is keeping the books, and He will deal justly with the giver and the receiver. Your responsibility is to give, and let the Lord take care of the rest.

John Wanamaker, a millionaire, once made a trip to China to determine how well the money he had given to missions was being used. He came upon an old man plowing with a crude instrument. It was drawn by an ox and a young man with a shining face. Asking for an explanation, he was told that the chapel needed a spire to be visible for miles around. The members had prayed, but the money was not enough. Then the son had said, "Let us sell one of our oxen and I will take the yoke of the ox we sell." Wanamaker prayed, "Lord, let me be hitched to a plow, so that I may know the joy of sacrificial giving."

This morning as I talked with my cover artist, he mentioned to me that God's system really works. He said the Lord had told him to give a certain missionary $100.00 for a project in his country of labor. Nick did not have the money, but he gave it anyway. He said his mother-in-law came to their house right after that and bought them a car battery they needed and $300.00 worth of new bedding. He said since he has operated in God's economy, God is just pouring in the blessings. God has it for you. You do not have to rely on the world system. You just have to obey Him and do it correctly. (Many people do not, and then wonder why it doesn't work.)

Remember the next time you give that God loves a cheerful giver. You may say, "I thought God loved everyone." He does, but not everyone pleases Him. If you want to please God and have His approval instead of His disapproval, think long and hard on this chapter. There may need to be some readjustment to your giving habits. God gives His blessing on one giver, and then rejects the offering of another (Cain and Abel). He has a right way to do things. It is for us to study and discover the right way, so as not to incur His wrath.

When David wanted to bring the ark back to Jerusalem, he and his people set the ark of God upon a new cart, and brought it out of the house of Abinadab in Gibeah. They were going along when suddenly the ark started to fall over, and Uzzah put forth his hand and took hold of it. "And the anger of the Lord was kindled against Uzzah; and God smote him there for his error; and there he died by the ark of God" (II Samuel 6:7).

God had a right way to carry the ark, but it was up to David to find out how. He discovered that none could carry the ark of God but the Levites because God had chosen them to do so. So this time when they went for the ark, "The children of the Levites bare the ark of God upon their shoulders with the staves thereon, as Moses commanded according to the word of the Lord" (I Chronicles 15:15).

Yes, God does give approval or disapproval. He has one way to do things, and it is for us to find out His proper way. Have you been giving properly? Has your attitude been cheerful towards giving the tithe and offerings, or has it been begrudging and miserly? Only you truly know; only you with God's help can change it, so you can receive His blessing.

START DOING THIS AND BE BLESSED

Before going to Section II, please read the following scripture passage. Then read the modern version of what you should say or think in your heart every time you bring your tithe or offering to God.

DEUTERONOMY 26:1-11

1. And it shall be, when thou art come in unto the land which the LORD thy God giveth thee for an inheritance, and possessest it, and dwellest therein;

2. That thou shalt take of the first of all the fruit of the earth, which thou shalt bring of thy land that the LORD thy God giveth thee, and shalt put it in a basket, and shalt go unto the place which the LORD thy God shall choose to place his name there.

3. And thou shalt go unto the priest that shall be in those days, and say unto him, I profess this day unto the LORD thy God, that I am come unto the country which the LORD sware unto our fathers for to give us.

4. And the priest shall take the basket out of thine hand, and set it down before the altar of the LORD thy God.

5. And thou shalt speak and say before the LORD thy God, A Syrian ready to perish was my father, and he went down into Egypt, and sojourned there with a few, and became there a nation, great, mighty, and populous:

6. And the Egyptians evil entreated us, and afflicted us, and laid upon us hard bondage:

7. And when we cried unto the LORD God of our fathers, the LORD heard our voice, and looked on our affliction, and our labour, and our oppression:

8. And the LORD brought us forth out of Egypt with a mighty hand, and with an outstretched arm, and with great terribleness, and with signs, and with wonders:

9. And he hath brought us forth out of Egypt with a mighty hand, and with an outstretched arm, and with great terribleness, and with signs, and with wonders:

10. And now, behold, I have brought the firstfruits of the land, which thou, O LORD, hast given me. And thou shalt set it before the LORD thy God, and worship before the LORD thy God:

11. And thou shalt rejoice in every good thing which the LORD thy God hath given unto thee, and unto thine house, thou, and the Levite, and the stranger that is among you.

GIVING IN ACTION

Now, friend, when you come before the Lord with your tithe and offering, say something of this nature:

"I was afflicted, ready to perish, in bondage, and full of fear. When I cried unto the LORD God of our fathers, the LORD heard my voice, and looked upon my affliction.

"He delivered me and brought me forth with a mighty hand; and with signs and wonders He has revealed Himself. The LORD has brought me into His kingdom where spiritual milk and honey flow.

"Now, behold, I have brought my tithes and offering, the first of all my increase that thou, O LORD hast given me.

"And now I worship you, O God and rejoice in every good thing which thou hast given unto me!"

Section II

INTEGRITY

Integrity means to be honest with self, God and others-no double life. It is a state or quality of being complete, undivided; unimpaired; moral soundness, honesty, and freedom from corrupting influence or practice. It is strictness in the fulfillment of contracts.

It pays to live right, for sin always has a way of finding a person out. This happened to a pirate ship a little over a century ago, when pirates roamed over the seas between the southern states. The Spanish main, the brig, Nancy was being pursued by the British warship, Sparrow. She was suspected of being engaged to illicit trade and piracy, but when captured, not a scrap of incriminating evidence could be found among her papers. It was thought that she should have to be released, but the question was referred to the authorities at Kingston, Jamaica, so into her port she was brought.

Meanwhile another vessel, a tender of the British frigate, Abergavenny, had been cruising in the same waters. One day, off the coast of Haiti, the officer in charge noticed a dead bullock in the water, surrounded by sharks. He gave orders for the bullock to be towed alongside the boat, and by this means the men succeeded in catching one of the sharks. It proved to be an unusually large one, and when opened, a parcel of papers tied round with string was discovered in its stomach.

These papers which can still be seen in the Institute Museum of Jamaica were found to relate to the doings of a ship called the Nancy, and thinking that they might serve a useful purpose, the officer preserved them till he reached Kingston, which was his next port of call. He arrived there just as the Nancy came before the courts.

The consternation of the Nancy's captain and crew may be imagined, when, jubilant at the prospect of release, they were suddenly confronted with the misdeeds found in the papers which they had thrown overboard when pursued by the warship--papers which they thought were buried in the depths of the sea.

God just happened to have that shark there at the particular time, and He just happened to have that dead bullock there to attract the attention of the captain who just happened to be going to Kingston where the trial was being held. It did not just happen; God ordered it.

The next four chapters deal with integrity in giving forgiveness, giving blessing in speech, in giving service, and in purity. All four require integrity, honesty, and strict adherence to that which is right.

Chapter 8

GIVE PURITY

This generation needs examples of purity. One of the knights of King Arthur's Round Table was Sir Galahad, called the "Maiden Knight" because of his pure life. Tennyson reports him as saying, "My strength is as the strength of ten, because my heart is pure." Purity gives strength.

The stables of Augeas, King of Elis, in Greece are legendary. In these stables he had kept 3,000 oxen and the stalls had not been cleansed for thirty years. When Hercules was appointed to clean these stables, he caused two rivers to run through them. Thus to cleanse the Augean stables means to clear away an accumulated mass of corruption, be it moral, religious, physical, or legal.

I say it is time to clean the stables. Let Calvary's flow of blood sweep over this generation, run through the churches, homes, schools, and governments. Corruptness is abounding, homosexuality is increasing, violence is on the uprise, but where sin doth abound, grace does much more abound.

The purity of honesty is lost in some circles. Fraud and cheating has become a way of life, but it still does not make it right. The world needs examples that make a shining pathway for them to follow.

A young minister preached one morning on the text, "Thou shalt not steal." The next morning he stepped on the bus and handed the driver a dollar bill. The driver handed him back his change. He stood in the rear of the bus and counted the change. There was a dime too much. His first thought was, "The bus company will never miss the dime."

Then quickly came the realization that he could not keep money that did not belong to him. He made his way to the front and said to the driver, "You gave me too much change."

Imagine his surprise when the driver replied, "Yes, a dime too much. I gave it to you purposely. You see, I heard your sermon yesterday, and I watched in my mirror as you counted your change. Had you kept the dime I would never again have had any confidence in preaching."

It is possible to live in the midst of greed, blackmail and extortion and remain untouched as a beacon to those following and watching you. It is like a water spider found in Europe. It forms a bubble about itself in which, like a diving bell, it sinks to the bottom of a pond or river. It will remain there for hours, living below, and yet breathing the air from above. When it returns to the surface it is found to be perfectly dry. Not the slightest moisture will have penetrated its capsule. It is in the water and yet separate from it, maintained by contact with the beyond.

How like the spider we should be. Our lifeline is connected to the heavenly world which has a different set of
rules to live by. We breathe from the oxygen of the Bible,
and it forms a capsule around us that keeps out evil
influence. We have the power to influence our world, as
Joseph did, instead of our world influencing us. Joseph
kept his integrity and purity even when the mistress of the
house tempted him. His purity took him to the top and he
became second-in-command to the Pharaoh.

A minister was approached by one of the members of
his congregation--a doctor--who offered him theater tickets. He said, "Take these. You need the recreation of
going and seeing this play." His pastor looked at them.
Seeing they were tickets to a play of the kind he could not
conscientiously attend, he said kindly, "Thank you, but I
cannot take them. I can't go."

"Why not?" the physician asked.

"Doctor, it's this way. You're a physician; a surgeon, in
fact. When you operate, you scrub your hands meticulous-
ly until you are especially clean. You would not dare
operate with dirty hands. I'm a servant of Christ. I deal
with precious human souls. I wouldn't dare to do my
service with a dirty life."

This generation needs clean hands. Husbands and
wives need to keep themselves for one another. If either
one has eyes for another, it is sin and needs to be dealt with
immediately, before it becomes a snare. Build up your
marriage, love one another, and quit desiring someone
else. The devil is out to get you and is working on your
marriage. Make it clean; don't let Satan win. Stand up

and fight for what God gave you. "A prudent man forseeth the evil, and hideth himself: but the simple pass on, and are punished" (Proverbs 22:3). Do not let the enemy punish you. Be wise instead of dumb. Those bright lights and flirtatious ways of another will only lead to damnation. Hide yourself in each other's arms and in the Rock of Ages. Get smart and realize that your marriage is a trust to be preserved.

Hand down to your kids a good name. At a social function, J.C. Penney, the merchant prince, took ginger ale, and someone mistakenly reported that he drank a cocktail. So he said, "I am sure that a reputation which I value has been endangered by my drinking ginger ale. Hereafter it will be plain water or tomato juice for me." "A good name is rather to be chosen than great riches, and loving favour rather than silver and gold" (Proverbs 22:1).

The story is told about a man named Joe that everybody loved. One night at a little mission a preacher gave an invitation for those that needed God to come down to the altar and pray. Down the aisle came an old bum, and when the preacher went to pray with him, he heard him saying over and over, "Dear Lord, make me like Joe."

The preacher said, "Ask God to make you like Jesus."

The bum opened his eyes and looked at the preacher in astonishment, then asked, "Was Jesus any better than Joe?" Everybody in that area loved Joe. Only the Master knows how many men Joe led to Christ. Joe had been buried that afternoon and the bums of the Bowery wept.

Would those that know us and do not know Jesus be able to ask, "Is Jesus any better than Joe?" Is our life lived with simple honesty and purity? Do we touch people with the true gospel of love and care? Do they want to be like us?

Chapter 9

GIVE FORGIVENESS

Forgive means to give, to resign or to cease to feel resentment against, on account of wrong committed, or to pardon.

Phillips Brooks, the minister who wrote the poem, *O Little Town of Bethlehem* which was later set to music, gave this address to his church one Sunday morning as he pled for brotherly love:

"You who are letting miserable misunderstandings run on from year to year, meaning to clear them up some day:

"You who are keeping wretched quarrels alive because you cannot quite make up your mind that now is the day to sacrifice your pride and kill them;

"You who are passing men sullenly upon the street, not speaking to them out of some silly spite, and yet knowing that it would fill you with shame and remorse if you heard that one of those men were dead tomorrow morning;

"You who are letting your neighbor starve, till you hear that he is dying from starvation;

"Or letting your friend's heart ache for a word of appreciation or sympathy, which you mean to give him someday;

"If you only could know and see and feel, all of a sudden, that the time is short, how it would break the spell! How you would go instantly and do the thing which you might never have another chance to do.

"Forgive. Forget. Bear with the faults of others as you would have them bear with yours. Be patient and understanding. Life is too short to be vengeful or malicious."

As the congregation poured out of the church that Sunday morning, people who hadn't spoken in years suddenly smiled and greeted each other and discovered it was what they had been wanting to do all along. Neighbors who had disliked and avoided each other walked home together and were astonished to find how they enjoyed doing it.

On March 4, 1865, President Abraham Lincoln stepped out on the inauguration platform on the east front of the Capitol and faced a vast sea of humanity. He ended his speech with these eloquent words:

"With malice toward none; with charity for all; with firmness in the right, as God gives us to see the right, let us strive on to finish the work we are in; to bind up the nation's wounds; to care for him who shall have borne the battle, and for his widow and his orphan."

Lincoln did not believe in harboring resentments or bearing grudges. He never realized the impact his speech would have on his country down through the years. It is a message of forgiveness and caring, a living principle of action.

To not forgive is never justified. Jesus said to forgive seventy times seven every day. The person hurt the worse by an unforgiving spirit is the one who will not forgive. The prolonged resentment and anger causes disease, headaches, and a general unrest. John Greenleaf Whittier gave to us the following poem that says it well:

My heart was heavy, for its trust had been
Abused, its kindness answered with foul wrong;
So turning gloomily from my fellow men,
One summer Sabbath day I strolled among
The green mounds of the village burial-place;
Where, pondering how all human love and hate
Find one sad level; and how, soon or late,
Wronged and wrongdoer, each with meekened face,
And cold hands folded over a still heart,
Pass the green threshold of our common grave,
Whither all footsteps tend, whence none depart,
Awed for myself, and pitying my race,
Our common sorrow, like a mighty wave,
Swept all my pride away, and, trembling, I forgave!

Forgiveness is hindered by our foolish pride. We harbor wrong thoughts and with them comes despair. There is nothing that takes the joy out of life like unconfessed sin on the conscience. The story was told about a young man who worked for a boat building company. He started to work on a boat in his own yard after hours, and started taking copper nails home from work with him. The nails were quite expensive and he knew he was stealing, but he would try to salve his conscience by telling himself that the boss had so many he would never miss them. After hearing a minister preach on covering sin, he went to the preacher and said, "This sermon has brought me face to face with myself and made me realize I am just a common thief. But I cannot go to my boss and tell him what I have done or offer to pay for those I have used and return the rest. If I do he will think I am just a hypocrite. And yet those copper nails are digging into my conscience and I know I shall never have peace until I put this matter right."

For weeks the struggle went on. Then one night he went to his pastor and exclaimed, "Pastor, I've settled for the copper nails and my conscience is relieved at last."

"What happened when you confessed to your employer what you had done?" asked the pastor.

"Oh," he answered, "he looked queerly at me, then exclaimed, 'George, I always did think you were just a hypocrite, but now I begin to feel there's something in this Christianity after all. Any religion that would make a dishonest workman come back and confess that he had been stealing copper nails and offer to settle for them, must be worth having.' "

Pride kept him from confessing for quite awhile, but when he finally broke down and just did it, a great load lifted from his conscience. Everyone was blessed and his boss forgave him. Do not let pride keep you from making things right.

Jesus said, "For if ye forgive men their trespasses, your heavenly Father will also forgive you: But if ye forgive not men their trespasses, neither will your Father forgive your trespasses" (Matthew 6:14-15).

We want the blessing of prayers answered and financial needs met, but it has an "if" to it. Jesus said in Mark 11 that if we asked for anything and had faith that we would receive it; but He also said along with that, to forgive. He said, "When ye stand praying, forgive, if ye have ought against any: that your Father also which is in heaven may forgive you your trespasses. But if ye do not forgive, neither will your Father which is in heaven forgive your trespasses" (Mark 11:25-26).

Dale Carnegie said, "When we hate our enemies, we are giving them power over us: power over our sleep, our appetites, our blood pressure, our health, and our happiness. Our enemies would dance with joy if only they knew how they were worrying us, lacerating us, and getting even with us! Our hate is not hurting them at all, but our hate is turning our own days and nights into a hellish turmoil."

To forgive is not easy, but it is the only way to blessing. The best example of forgiving an enemy is expressed in the following story. During the Revolutionary War there lived in Pennsylvania a pastor by the name of Peter Miller. Although Miller was greatly loved by everyone in the community, there was one man who lived near the church who hated him and had earned a reputation for his abuse of the minister. The man was not only a hater of the church, but he turned out to be a traitor to his country and was sentenced to die.

The trial was conducted in Philadelphia, and no sooner did Miller hear of it than he set out on foot to visit General Washington and interceded for the man's life. But Washington told him, "I'm sorry that I cannot grant your request for your friend."

"Friend!" Miller cried, "Why, that man is the worst enemy I have in the world!"

"What?" the general exclaimed in surprise. "Have you walked sixty miles to save the life of an enemy? That, in my judgement, puts the matter in a different light. I will grant him a pardon for your sake."

The pardon was made out and signed by General Washington, and Miller proceeded at once on foot to a place fifteen miles distant where the execution was scheduled to take place that afternoon. He arrived just as the man was being carried to the scaffold, and when he saw Miller hurrying toward the place, remarked, "There is old Peter Miller. He has walked all the way from Ephrata to have his revenge today by seeing me hung." But scarcely had he spoken the words when Miller pushed his way through to the condemned man and handed him the pardon that saved his life.

Jesus on an old rugged cross, feeling pain, rejection, and humiliation, looked on His accusers and those that mocked Him and cried, "Father, forgive them; for they know not what they do..." (Luke 23:34). If Jesus could forgive, and if we have His spirit within, we can forgive. It is said, "To err is human; to forgive is divine." Only Christ can give a person the capability to forgive and forget, but it is possible. He who forgives most, will be forgiven most. Give and it shall be given unto you.

How do you forgive? Jesus said to talk it out in meekness.

Therefore if thou bring thy gift to the altar, and there rememberest that thy brother hath ought against thee; Leave there thy gift before the altar, and go thy way; first be reconciled to thy brother...Agree with thine adversary quickly, whiles thou art in the way with him (Matthew 5:23-25).

Be careful not to argue. Humble yourself and remember there is more than one way to look at something. What does it mean to reconcile? *Reconcile* means to cause to be friendly again; to restore to friendship; to bring back to harmony.

What if someone has done you a deep wrong in your childhood or marriage--a total injustice--that you feel has scarred you emotionally? You ask, "Can I forgive?" I answer, "No, you cannot forgive on your own. The hurt is too deep." You may not be able to in yourself, but I know Jesus can help you to be able to forgive. He came just for that purpose. He came to bind up the broken hearted, to set the captives free from the prisons of hurt in which they are encased. It is the miracle of Calvary. Because He came, you can forgive; but only through Him. Not by your might, nor by your power, but by His spirit, are you able to forgive.

One sure way to forgive and forget is to become absorbed in some cause that is bigger than yourself. When your mind is filled with excitement over something that enthuses your thinking facilities, you do not have time to brood and think negative thoughts. "An idle mind is the devil's workshop."

Start praying today for wisdom and understanding to know how to forgive. He will tell you what to do. He has all the answers and He is liberal with His wisdom. Ask of Him today and He will help you.

Chapter 10

GIVE BLESSING

The following story, called *Pass on the Praise*, was found in a hundred-year-old book:

"You're a great little wife, and I don't know what I would do without you." And as he spoke he put his arms about her and kissed her, and she forgot all the care in that moment. And, forgetting it all, she sang as she washed the dishes, and sang as she made the beds and the song was heard next door, and a woman there caught the refrain and sang also, and two homes were happier because he had told her that sweet old story--the story of the love of a husband for a wife. As she sang, the butcher boy who called for the order heard it and went out whistling on his journey, and the world heard the whistle, and one man hearing it thought, "Here is a lad who loves his work, a lad happy and contented."

So, because he kissed her and praised her, the song came and the influence went out and out. And because she sang her heart was mellowed, and as she swept about the back door the cool air kissed her on each cheek, and she thought of a poor old woman she knew, and a little basket went over to that home with a quarter for a crate or two of wood.

Pass on the praise.

A word and you make a rift in the cloud, a smile and you may create a new resolve, a grasp of the hand and you may repossess a soul from hell.

Pass on the praise.

Does your clerk do well?

Pass on the praise.

Tell him that you are pleased and if he is a good clerk he will appreciate it.

Pass on the praise.

Don't go to the grave and call, "Mother." Don't plead, "Hear me, mother; you were a kind mother; you were a good mother, and smoothed away many a rugged path for me."

Those ears cannot hear that glad admission. Those eyes cannot see the light of earnestness in yours. Those hands may not return the embrace you now wish to give. Why call too late? Pass on the praise today.

From that same book came these words by Mary Cholmondeley: "Every year I live I am more convinced that the waste of life lies in the love we have not given, the powers we have not used, the selfish prudence that will risk nothing, and which, shirking pain, misses happiness as well. No one ever yet was the poorer in the long run for having once in a lifetime 'let out all the length of all the reins.' "

It is time to live as if every person we meet would be our family or someone that would live next to us. Let strangers be treated roughly no more, but spread blessing. Give blessing, speak blessing, do something that will bless others. Ruskin said it this way: "It's a good safe rule to sojourn in every place as if you meant to spend your life there, never omitting an opportunity of doing a kindness, speaking a true word or making a friend."

You curse people when you gossip about them. It not only curses the person that is talked about, the curse comes on the gossiper. James said, "And the tongue is a fire, a world of iniquity: so is the tongue among our members, that it defileth the whole body, and setteth on fire the course of nature; and it is set on fire of hell" (James 3:6).

The story is told of a peasant with a troubled conscience who had come to a monk for advice. The peasant had circulated slander about a friend--only to find out later that it wasn't true.

The sage was old and wise and said, "If you want to make peace with your conscience, you must fill a bag with chicken down, go to every dooryard in the village, and drop in each of them one fluffy feather."

The peasant did as he was told. Then he came back to the monk and announced that he had done penance for his folly. "Not yet!" said the sage sternly. "Take up your bag, go the rounds again, and gather up every feather that you have dropped."

"But the wind must have blown them all away," he said. "Yes, my son," replied the sage. "And so it is with gossip. Words are easily dropped, but no matter how hard you try, you can never get them back again."

Peter said,

Finally, be all of one mind, having compassion one of another, love as brethren, be pitiful, be courteous: Not rendering evil for evil, or railing for railing: but contrariwise blessing; knowing that ye are thereunto called, that ye should inherit a blessing. For he that will love life, and see good days, *let him refrain his tongue from evil, and his lips that they speak no guile* (I Peter 3:8-10).

Speak a blessing today and every day if you want to receive a blessing, for whatever comes out of you will come back to you increased. If you want to be blessed, bless others. The Earl of Shaftesbury said, "During a long life I have proved that not one kind word ever spoken, not one kind deed ever done, but sooner or later returns to bless the giver, and becomes a chain, binding men with golden bands to the throne of God."

It was said by Benjamin Disraeli, "Life is too short to be little." It is time to open our hearts and speak words of life and edification; time to choose life, love, and understanding before it is too late.

Do not keep the alabaster boxes of your love and tenderness sealed up until your friends are dead. Fill their lives with sweetness. Speak approving, cheering words while their ears can hear them and while their hearts can be thrilled by them (Henry Ward Beecher).

There are not enough people blessing others. Negative words flow most frequently. If anything is wrong, the world will hear about it quickly, but let a good deed be done, and many times it goes unnoticed. This day let your tongue be filled with sweetness. Look for something for which to bless others. To give a blessing is to bless yourself as well as the one blessed. There is power in blessing.

These three readings were taken from the book, *Field of Diamonds*:

BEAUTY OF LANGUAGE
Author unknown

There is a beauty of language, just as there is a beauty of face. There is a harmony of words, just as there is a harmony of sky and stars, green foliage, and crystal waters. There is a delicacy of speech, just as there is a delicacy of tints in the masterpiece on canvas, in the shimmer of light on the dewdrop, in the semi-transparent petal of the woodland flower.

WATCH YOUR WORDS
Author unknown

Keep a watch on your words, my darlings,
For words are wonderful things;
They are sweet, like the bees' fresh honey,
Like the bees, they have terrible stings.
They can bless like the warm, glad sunshine,
And brighten a lonely life;
They can cut, in the strife of anger,
Like an open, two-edged knife.

PASS IT ON
Henry Burton

Have you had a kindness shown?
Pass it on;
Twas not given for thee alone,
Pass it on;
Let it travel down the years,
Let it wipe another's tears,
Till in Heaven the deed appears--
Pass it on.

Get involved in blessing people. How many friends, ministers, teachers, grocers--the list is endless--have done something to encourage you, help you or inspire you? How many of them have you thanked? It is time to get out of yourself and start writing some thank you notes, letters, and cards. It is time to call the florist and send some flowers to those loved and appreciated. You think kind thoughts about someone and mention them to someone else; it is time to say them to the one you appreciate. Bless others. Benjamin Franklin said, "When you are good to others, you are best to yourself." It was Zoroaster that said, "Doing good to others is not a duty. It is a joy, for it increases your own health and happiness."

Moses spoke to the children of Israel these words God had given him, but they apply to us today:

Behold, I set before you this day a blessing and a curse; A blessing, if ye obey the commandments of the Lord your God, which I command you this day; And a curse, If ye will not obey the commandments of the Lord your God... (Deuteronomy 11:26-28).

Peter told us that if we wanted the blessing, we must bless others with our mouth. We alone will choose the blessing or the curse.

We must not only bless one another, but we must bless the Lord. He is the first one that should receive the blessing. David sang, "I will bless the Lord at all times: his praise shall continually be in my mouth" (Psalm 34:1). With His praise in our mouth, how can we gossip about each other? The attitude of the early church was one of blessing the Lord. When Jesus ascended to glory, where did you find the eleven?

And it came to pass, while he *blessed* them, he was parted from them, and carried up into heaven. And they worshipped him, and returned to Jerusalem with great joy: And were continually in the temple, praising and *blessing* God. Amen (Luke 24:51-53).

Start blessing the Lord. Start admiring, finding the good in people, and comment on it. Lift people up in this sinking world. Speak hope and cheer instead of doubt and dread. Give a blessing, and the blessings will come back to you. It is God's law: whatever you send out, it will return!

Chapter 11

GIVE SERVICE

The happiest people in the world are those who are living for others. The most miserable people in the world are those who live and think only of themselves. Become a tool in the Master's hand to serve a generation that needs love, understanding, and Christ.

Over and over in the Bible the word *service* is mentioned in connection with the temple or tabernacle--the place where God dwelt. "Their brethren also the Levites were appointed unto all manner of *service* of the tabernacle of the house of God" (I Chronicles 6:48). These were the priesthood. Also, others gave service to the house of God. When David was talking to Solomon and encouraging him to build the temple, he said,

And, behold, the courses of the priests and the Levites, even they shall be with thee for all the service to the house of God: and there shall be with thee for all manner of workmanship every willing skilful man, for any manner of *service:* also the princes and all the people will be wholly at thy commandment (I Chronicles 28:21).

Paul wrote to the Romans these words for us all:

I beseech you therefore, brethren, by the mercies of God, that ye present your bodies a living sacrifice, holy, acceptable unto God, which is your reasonable service (Romans 12:1).

It is time for more people to get involved in the service that concerns the house of the Lord--honest, humble service that will further the cause of Christ. When the pastor asks for workers for a certain cause, be the first to raise your hand to volunteer. If you want the blessing of the Lord, start giving yourself to His kingdom, not only in money, but in service.

Serve your church in labors, but also serve in helping others. The church was commended because of this. "For the administration of this service not only supplieth the want of the saints, but is abundant also by many thanksgivings unto God" (II Corinthians 9:12).

Phillips Brooks gives the following wisdom: "Look at the artist's chisel. The artist cannot carve without it. Yet imagine the chisel--conscious that it was made to carve--trying to carve alone. It lays itself against the hard marble, but it has neither strength nor skill. Then we can imagine the chisel full of disappointment. 'Why cannot I carve?' it cries. Then the artist comes and seizes it. The chisel lays itself into his hand, and is obedient to him. That obedience is faith. It opens the channels between the sculptor's brain and the hard steel. Thought, feeling, imagination, skill, flow down from the deep chambers of the artist's soul to the chisel's edge. The sculptor and the chisel are not two, but one; it is the unit which they make that carves the stone.

"We are but the chisel to carve God's statues in this world. Unquestionably we must do the work. But the human worker is only the chisel of the great Artist. The artist needs his chisel; but the chisel can do nothing, produce no beauty, of itself. The artist must seize it, and the chisel lay itself into his hand and be obedient to him. We must yield ourselves altogether to Christ and let Him use us. Then His power, His wisdom, His skill, His thought, His love, shall flow through our soul, our brain, our heart, our fingers. That is working by faith."

Giving service is giving influence. Your name is on the line. You sign your name to your work, or your endeavor. The reputation of a thousand years may be determined by the conduct of one hour, so live life well.

Whatever service or labor you give will be rewarded. Paul speaks to the Corinthians about this concept. He said, "...every man shall receive his own reward according to his own labour" (I Corinthians 3:8b).

You can sometimes give service and feel unappreciated or unrewarded, but you can rest assured that you will receive a reward. So the story goes about a middle-aged clerk in a large wholesale house. He had been there for 25 years, and for the last ten had occupied the first chair in the head office. During all these years he had been happy and contented, giving himself fully to his work, and to his church and Sunday School. Lately, however, a restlessness had been stealing into his heart and with it a desire for change. Something seemed to tell him his life was a wasted one because it had not been wider and greater.

The other clerks had all left the warehouse, so he bent his head upon his arms and when he lifted it there were hot tears in his eyes. His was the burning of the soul which consumes the vital energies and leaves a man powerless.

He started as someone opened the outer doors. It was the postman with the belated mail. Mechanically he gathered it up. There were two letters addressed to himself, one from the city, one from British Columbia. He opened the latter first and glanced at the signature. It was from a young man who had been under him for five years, and who two years ago had left for the West. It ran as follows:

Dear Mr. G---: I am writing to thank you for all your goodness to me while in your office. I am succeeding beyond my best expectations in business, and yesterday I became a member of the Church, having found Christ two months ago. For these two blessings of God I owe all to you, for in both business and religion you have been my example. I hope in this new land to help others as you have helped me.

The other was from one of his old Sunday School scholars, and read:

Dear Sir: I have taken your advice and once more feel I am a free man. With the money you loaned me I have paid my debts, and with God's help and yours will redeem the past. I cannot thank you as I ought; but I do trust that I will be worthy of your confidence.

A new light came into his face. The old restlessness passed forever. He walked with the step of his youth. God had held the goblet of life to his lips, and he had drunk deep. God knew just the right moment to give encouragement to a faithful servant.

Your service is important. Treat it with integrity and dignity. You may not be a star for all the world to see, but if you are doing your job well and helping other people, you are important to the continuity of God's plan.

In the same chapter of Romans, Paul had this to say concerning business: "Be...not slothful in business; fervent in spirit; serving the Lord; Recompense to no man evil for evil. Provide things honest in the sight of all men" (Romans 12:11:17).

When you take that apart, there are several key words: slothful, fervent, serving, recompense, and honest.

SLOTHFUL means laziness; idleness; to neglect or delay.

FERVENT means hot, glowing, warmth in feeling; ardent, passionate or eager in temperament.

SERVING is to be of use, to labor.

RECOMPENSE is to return in kind or to pay back.

HONEST is characterized by integrity or fairness and straightforwardness in conduct, thought, speech; upright, trustworthy.

Provide honest service for your employer. Do not be a clock-watcher; become a character watcher. Do not steal from the closet little things that belong to the company. Dishonesty is a severe paymaster. Provide all things honest in the sight of your fellow employees and your employers. Abraham Lincoln felt it was so important to return a few pennies that he had overcharged a woman for tea, that he walked six miles one way to return them to her after he finished his work. That same integrity and honesty in service took him to the White House.

Servants, be obedient to them that are your masters according to the flesh, with fear and trembling, in singleness of your heart, as unto Christ; Not with eyeservice, as menpleasers; but as the servants of Christ, doing the will of God from the heart; With good will doing service, as to the Lord, and not to men; Knowing that whatsoever good thing any man doeth, the same shall he receive of the Lord (Ephesians 6:5-8).

There it is in a nutshell. If you do your service unto the Lord, and remember that He sees all things, knows all things, and hears all things--and is keeping books--it will make you much more aware of honest service. The good part is this: Whatever good you do, the Lord will give it back to you. That should put a shout and a song in your heart, and make you want to roll up your sleeves and get to work--just looking for something to do. It is the best investment program I know!

In a church tower of a town in Germany there hangs a bell bearing the image of a six-eared stalk of corn, on which is the date October 15, 1729. The first bell hung in this tower was so small that its tones could not be heard at the end of the village. A new bell was needed, but the village was comprised of very poor people and money was not available.

One Sunday the schoolmaster noticed growing out of the church wall a green stalk of corn, the seed of which had been dropped by a passing bird. Suddenly he wondered if this stalk of corn could be made to produce the needed bell. He waited until the corn was ripe and he was able to pluck six ears, which he sowed in his garden. The next year he sowed his entire crop again. Lacking room, he divided with neighbors who continued to sow and reap from this corn for eight years. The money from this corn was taken to the church and kept in the fund for the new bell. At last the bell was bought and its story engraved on the side. We may not be able to do great things or bring large gifts, but if we lay at Jesus' feet the little we have, He will use it, multiply it and bless it.

This story represents what this book is about: sowing and reaping. The reason it is in the chapter on service is because one man did a service for a whole city by simply being diligent, observant, and caring. He served his church and he served his community. Everyone enjoyed the bell because of one soul on fire with a purpose. He could have passed on by and let the corn wither and die, but because he was a good steward, he produced corn many times over. It works! It is the Bible principle; you cannot improve on it. What can you give today? A little lunch fed 15,000 people. It does not matter the size of the gift, just do something with it instead of hoarding it. Serve and ye shall be served! Bless and ye shall be blessed. Give and it shall be given unto you!

Section III

VIRTVE

Jesus said virtue went out of His body when He gave healing to the little woman with the issue of blood. Virtue is to give part of self away. In the case of Jesus it was a supernatural power. Virtue is also moral practice or action, conformity to the standard of right: moral excellence, integrity of character, uprightness of conduct.

Plato distinguished four cardinal virtues: wisdom or prudence, courage or fortitude, temperance, and justice or righteousness. "Virtue is not to be considered in the light of mere innocence, or abstaining from harm, but as the exertion of our facilities in doing good" (Butler).

This section deals with giving to others, the principal of "Give and it shall be given," and the need for giving courage. Notice before you read Chapter 11, who we are to give to; based on Dueteronomy 26, Isaiah 58, and Galatians 6:

Deuteronomy 26
1. Levite (the ministry)
2. Stranger (new ones in the neighborhood, new ones in the Church, the friendless)
3. Fatherless

4. Widows

Isaiah 58
   1. Hungry
   2. Poor
   3. Homeless
   4. Naked

Galatians 6
   1. Saints or those in need in the
      household of faith

Chapter 12

GIVING TO OTHERS

"If you wish to be miserable, you must think about your-self, what you want, what you like, what respect people ought to pay you, and what people think of you" *(Author un-known)*.

"...For this thing the Lord will bless thee in all thy works, and in all that thou puttest thine hand unto" (Deuteron-omy 15:10). For what thing? For giving to the poor. Paraphrased, verses 7-10 say, "If there are any poor among you, do not harden your heart nor close your hand to them, but open your hand wide and give him sufficient for his need and anything he wants. While you are giving, do not be grieved about it, because you are actually blessing yourself by giving to them."

Whenever you give to the poor you are actually giving to the Master, for He said in Matthew 25, "Inasmuch as ye have done it unto the least of these, ye have done it unto me."

"He that hath pity upon the poor lendeth unto the Lord; and that which he hath given will he pay him again" (Proverbs 19:17).

Not giving to the poor is a serious sin. So serious that it caused a rich man to go to hell. The rich man fared sumptuously every day and was clothed in purple and fine linen. Outside his gate was a beggar named Lazarus, who had sores all over his body. All Lazarus asked for were the crumbs or leftovers, but the rich man would not give him anything. In time Lazarus died and the angels carried him to heaven, but when the rich man died he was buried. "And in hell he lift up his eyes, being in torments, and seeth Abraham afar off, and Lazarus in his bosom" (Luke 16:23).

How often we sin against the Lord by turning our face away from those that are in need. If we could only remember that we are not feeding only the poor, but we are actually doing it to the Lord Jesus Christ. That would erase the thought of worrying about the results of it.

If you have faith, but not works, it is not enough.

If a brother or sister be naked, and destitute of daily food, And one of you say unto them, Depart in peace, be ye warmed and filled; notwithstanding ye give them not those things which are needful to the body; what doth it profit? (James 2:15-16).

A well-to-do deacon in Connecticut was met one morning by his pastor, who said, "Poor Widow Green's wood is out. Can you not take her a cord?"

"Well," answered the deacon, "I have the wood and I have the team; but who is to pay me for it?"

The pastor replied, "I will pay you for it on condition that you read the first three verses of Psalm 41 before you go to bed tonight."

The deacon consented, delivered the wood, and at night opened the word of God and read the passage: "Blessed is he that considereth the poor; the Lord will deliver him in time of trouble. The Lord will preserve him and keep him alive; and he shall be blessed upon the earth; and thou wilt not deliver him unto the will of his enemies. The Lord will strengthen him upon the bed of languishing; thou wilt make all his bed in his sickness."

A few days afterward the pastor met him again. "How much do I owe you, deacon, for that cord of wood?"

"Oh," said the now-enlightened man, "do not speak of payment; I did not know those promises were in the Bible. I would not take money for supplying the widow's wants."

It is time to get addicted to the care of those in need. Paul talks about the house of Stephanas and "that they have addicted themselves to the ministry of the saints...I am glad of the coming of Stephanas and Fortunatus and Achaicus: for that which was lacking on your part they have supplied" (I Corinthians 16:15,17).

There is a curse pronounced upon them that will not give to the poor. God gave forth this command and the reason for it:

An Ammonite or Moabite shall not enter into the congregation of the Lord; even to their tenth genera-

tion shall they not enter into the congregation of the
Lord for ever: Because they met you not with bread
and water in the way, when ye came forth out of
Egypt... (Deuteronomy 23:3-4).

They were cursed because they did not supply a need.

"Liberality," says one, "is the most beneficial traffic that
can be. It is bringing our wares to the best market. It is
letting out our money into the best hands. We thereby
lend our money to God, who repays with vast usuary; an
hundred to one is the rate He allows at present, and above
a hundred millions to one He will render hereafter." Luke
18:30 tells us that he who has a sacrificial spirit shall
"receive manifold more in this present time, and in the
world to come life everlasting."

"What I saved I lost; what I spent I had; what I gave I
have," said J.J. Gurney.

We go our ways in life too much alone;
We hold ourselves too far from all our kind;
Too often we are dead to sigh and moan,
Too often to the weak and helpless blind;
Too often where distress and want abide
We turn and pass upon the other side.

Anonymous

The majority of those that passed the beaten man on the
road to Jericho passed to the other side. It was the
minority that stopped and ministered and gave of his
substance to the one that had less than him. Jesus asked

the question about the good Samaritan and said, "Which now of these three, thinkest thou, was neighbour unto him that fell among the thieves? And he said, He that shewed mercy on him. Then said Jesus unto him, Go, and do thou likewise" (Luke 10:36-37). It is not enough to see the need, but sight must motivate the heart to do something to better the situation.

Happiness is through helpfulness. Newell Dwight Hillis said, "Every morning let us build a booth to shelter some-one from life's fierce heat. Every noon let us dig some life-spring for thirsty lips."

Someone has said they never saw a U-Haul trailer hitched onto a hearse on the way to the burial place with the deceased. The things that you can take with you at the time of death are the things you have given away. The treasure in heaven consists of what involves the first and second greatest commandments: love the Lord God with all your soul, mind, spirit, and body; and love thy neighbor as thyself. Those things are waiting in heaven for you.

Happiness is doing for God and others. The things left undone are what causes the pain.

It isn't the thing you do dear,
It's the thing you left undone,
Which gives you a bit of heartache,
At the setting of the sun.
The tender word forgotten,
The letter you did not write.

The flower you might have sent, dear,
Are your haunting ghosts tonight.

Anonymous

We are commanded, "As we have therefore, let us do good unto all men, especially unto them who are of the household of faith" (Galatians 6:10). The Bible has much to say on this subject, but sometimes we just skip over it because of our own human reasoning. Do not worry about what you give or what will happen to that which you give. Just obey the word and for the most part it will be appreciated and people will be truly blessed. There are always a few hanger-ons and habitual lazy beggars, but do not let that stop you from obeying the scripture. The ones who do not deserve to be helped will eventually reveal themselves as you stay sensitive to God.

It is essential to minister to the poor or those that are struggling financially. Paul speaks about the attitude of the Macedonia church and their care for the poor: "But now I go unto Jerusalem to minister unto the saints. For it hath pleased them of Macedonia and Achaia to make certain contribution for the poor saints which are at Jerusalem" (Romans 15:25-26).

But whoso hath this world's good, and seeth his brother have need, and shutteth up his bowels of compassion from him, how dwelleth the love of God in him? My little children, let us not love in word, neither in tongue; but in deed and in truth (I John 3:17-18).

And above all things have fervent charity among yourselves...use hospitality one to another without grudging (I Peter 4:8,9).

Remember God is a good bookkeeper. "For God is not unrighteous to forget your work and labour of love, which ye have shewed toward his name, in that ye have ministered to the saints, and do minister" (Hebrews 6:10).
Paul exhorts in I Timothy,

Charge them that are rich in this world, that they be not highminded, nor trust in uncertain riches, but in the living God, who giveth us richly all things to enjoy; That they do good, that they be rich in good works, ready to distribute, willing to communicate; Laying up in store for themselves a good foundation against the time to come, that they may lay hold on eternal life (I Timothy 6:17-19).

This reminds us of the story of the rich young ruler. He had kept every commandment, but was unwilling to give his riches to others, thus forfeiting his right to eternal life. It is not enough to know the Lord Jesus Christ, but there is an obligation to do for those who are in need.
Paul commended the Macedonia church because they were the only church that fully understood true Christianity--that of giving and receiving. He said their gift was an odour of a sweet smell, a sacrifice acceptable, well-pleasing to God. (Philippians 4:18). He also shows what the outgrowth of love is. "Distributing to the necessity of

saints; given to hospitality" (Romans 12:13). You never lose by giving. You only lose by keeping.

When you hoard your goods, you will die either physically, emotionally, or spiritually. Mankind was made to give. You have to give to receive, spend to increase, plant to reap; it is the law of harvest. Whatever is given out will come back many times over. "Cast thy bread upon the waters: for thou shalt find it after many days" (Ecclesiastes 10:1). It shall come back.

In the city of Zarephath a widow woman and her son were going to eat their last little loaf of bread and then die. They were suffering greatly because of the famine, when suddenly Elijah appeared and asked her for a drink of water. He also asked her for a morsel of bread. She told him she did not have enough to give him, but Elijah told her not to fear. He said,

> ...Make me thereof a little cake first, and bring it unto me, and after make for thee and for thy son. For thus saith the Lord God of Israel, The barrel of meal shall not waste, neither shall the cruse of oil fail, until the day that the Lord sendeth rain upon the earth. And she went and did according to the saying of Elijah: and she, and he, and her house, did eat many days (I Kings 17:13-15).

She committed her future well-being to God's promises instead of economic circumstances. She gave of her lack and God pronounced a blessing upon her.

She gave and lived. She gave and received. She gave and blessed others. Not only did she bless herself, Elijah, and her son, but she blessed her whole household, including servants and other relatives as well. Giving to God and others always has rich returns. "...Whatsoever a man soweth, that shall he also reap" (Galatians 6:7).

A story told by a friend of Beethoven gives the history of the *Moonlight Sonata*, which has blessed the world with beautiful music. The inspiration for it came because Beethoven gave himself first. Following are the words of the nameless friend:

It happened at Bonn. One moonlight winter's evening I called upon Beethoven, for I wanted him to take a walk, and afterward sup with me. In passing through some dark, narrow street, he paused suddenly. "Hush!" he said. "What sound is that? It is from my sonata in F!" he said eagerly. "Hark! how well it is played!"

It was a little, mean dwelling, and we paused outside and listened. The player went on; but in the midst of the finale there was a sudden break, then the voice of sobbing. "I cannot play any more. It is so beautiful, it is utterly beyond my power to do it justice. Oh, what would I not give to go to the concert at Cologne!"

"Ah, my sister," said her companion, "why create regrets, when there is no remedy? We can scarcely pay our rent."

"You are right; and yet I wish for once in my life to hear some really good music. But it is of no use."

Beethoven looked at me. "Let us go in," he said.

"Go in!" I exclaimed. "What can we go in for?"

"I will play to her," he said in an excited tone. "Here is feeling, genius, understanding. I will play to her and she will understand it." And before I could prevent him his hand was upon the door.

A pale young man was sitting by the table making shoes; and near him, leaning sorrowfully upon an old-fashioned harpsichord, sat a young girl, with a profusion of light hair falling over her bent face. Both were cleanly but very poorly dressed, and both started and turned toward us as we entered.

"Pardon me," said Beethoven, "but I heard music, and was tempted to enter! I am a musician."

The girl blushed and the young man looked grave--somewhat annoyed.

"I also overheard something of what you said," continued my friend. "You wish to hear--that is you would like--that is--Shall I play for you?"

There was something so odd in the whole affair, and something so comic and pleasant in the manner of the speaker, that the spell was broken in a moment, and all smiled involuntarily.

"Thank you!" said the shoemaker, "but our harpsichord is so wretched, and we have no music."

"No music!" echoed my friend. "How then does the Fraulein..."

He paused and colored up, for the girl looked full at him, and he saw that she was blind.

"I--I entreat your pardon!" he stammered. "But I had not perceived before. Then you play by ear?"

"Entirely."

"And where do you hear the music, since you frequent no concerts?"

"I used to hear a lady practicing near us, when we lived at Bruhl two years. During the summer evenings her windows were generally open, and I walked to and fro outside to listen to her."

She seemed shy; so Beethoven said no more, but seated himself before the piano, and began to play. He had no sooner struck the first chord than I knew what would follow--how grand he would be that night. And I was not mistaken. Never, during all the years I knew him, did I hear him play as he then played to that blind girl and her brother. He was inspired; and from the instant when his fingers began to wander along the keys, the very tone of the instrument began to grow sweeter and more equal.

The brother and sister were silent with wonder and rapture. The former laid aside his work; the latter with her head bent slightly forward, and her hands pressed tightly over her breast, crouched down near the end of the harpsichord, as if fearful lest even the beating of her heart should break the flow of those magical, sweet sounds. It was as if we were all bound in a strange dream, and only feared to wake.

Suddenly the flame of the single candle wavered, sank, flickered, and went out. Beethoven paused, and I threw open the shutters, admitting a flood of brilliant moonlight. The room was almost as light as before, and the illumination fell strongest upon the piano and player. But the chain of his ideas seemed to have been broken by the accident. His head dropped upon his breast; his hands rested upon his knees; he seemed absorbed in meditation. It was thus for some time.

At length the young shoemaker rose and approached him eagerly, yet reverently. "Wonderful man!" he said, in a low tone, "Who and what are you?"

"Listen!" the composer said, and he played the opening bars of the sonata in F.

A cry of delight and recognition burst from them both, and exclaiming, "Then you are Beethoven?" they covered his hands with tears and kisses.

He rose to go, but we held him back with entreaties.

"Play to us once more--only once more!"

He suffered himself to be led back to the instrument. The moon shone brightly in through the window and lit up his glorious, rugged head and massive figure. "I will improvise a sonata to the moonlight!" looking up thoughtfully to the sky and stars. Then his hands dropped on the keys, and he began playing a sad and infinitely lovely movement, which crept gently over the instrument like the calm flow of moonlight over the dark earth.

This was followed by a wild, elfin passage in triple time--a sort of grotesque interlude. Then came a swift, agitato finale--a breathless, hurrying, trembling movement, descriptive of flight and uncertainty, and vague, impulsive terror, which carried us away on its rustling wings, and left us all in emotion and wonder.

"Farewell to you!" said Beethoven, pushing back his chair and turning toward the door, "farewell to you!"

"You will come again?" they asked in one breath.

He paused and looked compassionately, almost tenderly, at the face of the blind girl. "Yes, yes," he said hurriedly, "I will come again and give the Fraulein some lessons. Farewell! I will come again!"

They followed us in silence more eloquent than words, and stood at the door till we were out of sight and hearing.

"Let us make haste back," said Beethoven, "that I may write out that sonata while I can yet remember it."

We did so, and he sat over it till long past day-dawn. And this was the origin of that moonlight sonata with which we are all so fondly acquainted.

Give and it shall be given. Beethoven gave, and inspiration gave him the sonata. If he would not have given, there probably would not have been the sonata.

Proverbs says, "There is that scattereth, and yet increaseth; The liberal soul shall be made fat: and he that watereth shall be watered also himself" (Proverbs 11:24-25). As you bless others, you bless yourself. Ralph Waldo Emerson gave us these words: "Happiness is a perfume you cannot pour on others without getting a few drops on yourself."

Jesus said, "All things whatsoever ye would that men should do to you, do ye even so to them: for this is the law and the prophets" (Matthew 7:12). He knew and taught the principle-- whatever you give out will come back to you.

"Success is rooted in reciprocity. He who does not benefit the world is headed for bankruptcy on the high-speed clutch" (H.H. Rogers).

Chapter 13

GIVE AND IT SHALL BE GIVEN

Again and again we hear this scripture quoted in connection with money, but Jesus was not referring to money here, although the principle is true of monetary giving:

Give, and it shall be given unto you; good measure, pressed down, and shaken together, and running over, shall men give into your bosom. For with the same measure that ye mete withal it shall be measured to you again (Luke 6:38).

Notice that just prior to verse 38, verse 37 ends with a colon. That means that verse 38 is a continuation of a certain thought. What were the thoughts He emphasized before stating the popular scripture? What is He telling us to give? Needless to say, they are things we do not like to give. We want the benefits of doing these things, but we sure do not want to do them. They are:

1. Love your enemies, do good to them which hate you (verse 27).
2. Bless them that curse you (28).
3. Pray for them which despitefully use you (28).
4. Do good, and lend, hoping for nothing again (35).
5. Be merciful (36).
6. Judge not (37).
7. Condemn not (37).
8. Forgive (37).

What will happen if you do these things? According to verse 35, your reward will be great, and ye shall be the children of the Highest.

However, these things are impossible to do without His help. They are not normal. When people do you wrong, you want to hate them. You are glad when they fall and something bad happens to them. All the things He asks us to do are seemingly impossible, but He gives hope. In the same chapter He talks about the rock. He says that if we will hear and do what He tells us to do, that we would become like a man which built a house, and digged deep, and laid the foundation of a rock: and when the flood arose, the stream beat vehemently upon that house, and could not shake it: for it was founded upon a rock.

First step: Fall on the rock in humility and ask for His help. If we are arrogant and do it our own way then the rock will fall on us and grind us to powder (Luke 20:18). Paul said, "For though he was crucified through weakness, yet he liveth by the power of God. For we also are weak in him, but we shall live with him by the power of God toward you" (II Corinthians 13:4).

"Not that we are sufficient of ourselves to think any thing as of ourselves; but our sufficiency is of God" (II Corinthians 3:5).

Second step: Realize it is the power of God in us to help us do what He asks us to do. "Now thanks be unto God, which always causeth us to triumph in Christ..." (II Corinthians 2:14). We are made new and have a new nature. "Therefore if any man be in Christ, he is a new creature; old things are passed away; behold, all things are become new" (II Corinthians 5:17). He will help you do things that will astound you. "Now unto him that is able to do exceeding abundantly above all that we ask or think, according to the power that worketh in us" (Ephesians 3:20). His power is in you to do everything that is asked of you.

At a ladies retreat back East, a minister's wife gave her testimony concerning this very thing. She told how they had a little dog, and next door to them lived a man that was rather harsh and unfeeling. One day the dog came up missing and another neighbor told her that the man had killed their dog. She said every time she looked at that man she had rage and resentment towards him.

Not long after that her husband asked her to teach a series of lessons to the ladies at the church. She started teaching and as part of her studies read *May I Wash Your Feet*, a book on being a servant of Jesus Christ. She became so convicted about her attitude that she began to pray about it. The Lord spoke to her and told her to bake something and take it over to the man and apologize for her attitude.

The day finally came when she decided to do it. She baked a nice pie and then asked her husband to go over with her. He said, "No, the Lord told you to do it. You go on by yourself and I'll pray for you." So fearfully she walked up to the door and rang the bell. The little son answered the door and asked her to come in while he went to get his dad. She said she waited what seemed like a long time and when he finally showed up, she just blurted out, "I've had a grudge against you ever since my dog was killed, and I want to ask you to forgive me. Here's this pie for you also."

She said the funny thing about it was when she humbled herself and asked for forgiveness, he humbled himself and started apologizing also. They both left smiling and she said a great weight had been taken off her heart. Now she is free to witness to him about Jesus and His love because she obeyed Luke 6:38. She has never been happier or more blessed since she decided to do it God's way.

Knowing Christ changes you from getting even to giving instead. There were two families who lived side by side in the mountains of Kentucky and had been fighting and quarreling for years. The feud started when Grandfather Smith's cow jumped over the stone fence of Grandfather Brown and ate his corn. Brown shot the cow. During the ensuing fight, one of the Smith boys shot two of the Brown boys, while the Browns shot only one of the Smiths.

Bill, the oldest of the Brown family, wanted to even up matters, especially since it was his own father who had been killed. But Bill was called away to war. While he was away his mother had a hard time providing for the family.

One Christmas the head of the Smith family took his wife and children to church. Usually he stayed outside, but it was so cold he decided to go in and wait. The sermon was on Christ, the Prince of Peace. It struck Smith's heart. On his way home he passed the home of the Browns and he began to realize what a crime he had committed in killing the breadwinner. He prayed. He did more. He determined secretly to help them. He hired a small boy to carry a basket of food to the Browns every day.

When Bill came home and heard of this kindness, he decided to find out who the generous helper was. He followed the little boy to the door of Smith's house. He could not believe his eyes. When Smith answered his knock, he smiled and declared:

"Shoot me, Bill, if you want to."

But Bill said he had come to thank him for taking care of his family while he was gone. Then Smith explained to Bill how he had come to a change of heart. He had heard the story of the first Christmas, the story of the Prince of Peace. It changed him.

True giving does not make distinction. The heart of a giver gives to the lowly as well as the prince--whoever has a need. Unsightliness does not bother the giver. He gives to God and others because he cares and loves.

The story is told about Peter the Great, emperor of Russia, who was given to strange moods. At one time he decided to play the part of a beggar in a certain village. From door to door he tramped asking for help. Only one poor man showed him any kindness. The next day the royal carriage came to a stop before the door of that poor home, and the man who had befriended Peter the Great was invited to live in the palace at Moscow. Give and it shall be given, pressed down, shaken together, will men heap it into thy bosom!

Notice in the same passage of scripture, Luke 6:35-38, one phrase stands out: "He is kind." No one is ever too big to be kind. Lord Palmerston, Queen Victoria's Prime Minister, was crossing Westminster Bridge when a little girl ahead dropped a jug of milk. The jug broke into fragments, and she dissolved into tears. Palmerston, having no money with him, dried her eyes by telling her that if she came to the same spot next day at that hour he would pay for both jug and milk. The following morning, in the midst of a cabinet meeting, he suddenly remembered his promise to the little girl, left the bewildered ministers, dashed across the bridge, popped half a crown into the waiting child's hand and hurried back.

Kindness is a prerequisite for greatness. Many years ago Dwight W. Morrow, the father of Anne Lindbergh, told a group of friends that Calvin Coolidge had real presidential possibilities. They disagreed, saying that Coolidge was too quiet, and lacked color and political personality. "No one would like him," objected one of the group.

But up piped little Anne, then aged six: "I like Mr. Coolidge." Then she displayed a finger with a bit of adhesive tape on it. "He was the only one who asked me about my sore finger."

Mr. Morrow nodded. "There's your answer," he said. His kindness took him to the White House in 1923, and made him the 30th President of the United States.

Kindness pays great dividends. To ex-serviceman James Kilpatrick, of Glendale, California, it was everyday kindness to share his army coffee and cakes from home with a hungry old French lady. That kindness so impressed Mme. Jeanne Marshall, 83, of Baccarat, France, whose seven sons were killed by the Nazis, that she willed Kilpatrick $50,000 before her death. The bequest was totally unexpected to Kilpatrick--all for an act of kindness.

What do you want today? Do you want kindness? Do you want friends? Do you want mercy from others? Do you want a glow in your heart? If you do, you must start the chain of action. Whatever it is you want you must do it first. Plant a seed, reap a plant. Plant an acorn, reap an oak. "A man that hath friends must shew *himself* friendly..." (Proverbs 18:24). Plant a thought, reap an action. "For as he thinketh in his heart, so is he" (Proverbs 23:7). Nothing happens by itself; it is cause and effect. Get out of yourself; quit feeling sorry for yourself, and lose your self in the cause of Christ and helping others. Jesus said it. If you want to find life, you have to lose your life for His sake, a cause bigger than your own problems. The more you give the more you receive.

How much do you want? Then that's how much you have to give. You do not get something for nothing. It is seedtime. Go out today and start planting seeds and sure as the sun rises, they will come up. You are the gardener--you choose the seeds. God has provided the soil and the elements, the Word and His spirit; and it shall come to pass just as He said it. Just as there is a natural harvest, there is a spiritual harvest. The Lord said, "While the earth remaineth, seedtime and harvest, and cold and heat, and summer and winter, and day and night shall not cease" (Genesis 8:22).

"In the morning sow thy seed, and in the evening withhold not thine hand: for thou knowest not whether shall prosper, either this or that, or whether they both shall be alike good" (Ecclesiastes 11:6). So when you get up in the morning, sow all day long, and sow in the evening, for there shall come a harvest. "As we have therefore opportunity, let us do good unto all men, especially unto them who are of the household of faith" (Galatians 6:10). Do good to all men--everyone you meet. Do not reserve your best manners for the church house. Do good in the market place, the mall, the post office, the DMV; everywhere you go *look* for opportunity to do good. When you are good to others, you are best to yourself. Make a conscious effort to do it today!

Chapter 14

GIVE COURAGE

Courage is that quality of mind which enables one to encounter danger and difficulties with firmness; valor, and boldness.

The Lord God is always positive. I like what He told Joshua when Moses died. Joshua had the awesome responsibility to take the place of Moses, one of the greatest leaders who ever lived. Joshua must have been feeling a little shaky, for the Lord told him to get up and be strong. He said, "Have not I commanded thee? Be strong and of a good courage; be not afraid, neither be thou dismayed: for the Lord thy God is with thee whithersoever thou goest" (Joshua 1:9).

As God instructed Joshua to be courageous, Joshua instructed those under him to have courage. Courage is contagious, the same way fear is. Fear is a disease among this generation, and it lurks in every corridor ready to pounce on its next victim. People harbor it, speak it, and practice it. It is time to do something about it. Fear is the opposite of courage. This is the day to have courage.

These are difficult times, but courage enables one to face danger with firmness and boldness.

Touch others this day with courage. May every soul that touches you, be it the slightest contact, get some good. May you give one spark of inspiration or gleam of faith that would fire them towards God and true life. Cease to have a ten-spy mentality; seek to have the two-spy mentality, which said, "...We are well able to overcome it" (Numbers 13:30). Have we forgotten who we are serving? Have we become disbelievers like the children of Israel? They did not have to wander forty years in the wilderness. They chose that route simply because they did not believe in the promises of God. They chose to listen to the doubters who said they were not able. It is time to speak courage and live it.

The following quotation is from the *Cadet Prayer* that has been repeated every Sunday in chapel services at West Point: "Make us choose the harder right instead of the easier wrong, and never to be contented with half truth when whole truth can be won. Endow us with courage that is born of loyalty to all that is noble and worthy, that scorns to compromise with vice and injustice and knows no fear when right and truth are in jeopardy."

Lincoln showed the quality of his courage, when against the advice of Congress, he made the call for an additional 500,000 recruits. He was told it would prevent his re-election. With flashing eye he replied, "It is not necessary for me to be re-elected, but it is necessary for the soldiers at the front to be reinforced by 500,000 men, and I shall call for them; and if I go down under the act, I will go down, like the Cumberland, with my colors flying."

It was Henry Clay who was about to introduce a certain bill in Congress when a friend said, "If you do, Clay, it will kill your chance for the presidency."

"But is the measure right?" Clay asked, and on being assured it was right, said, "I would rather be right than be president."

I like what Joab said at the time of a fierce battle: "Be of good courage, and let us behave ourselves valiantly for our people, and for the cities of our God: and let the Lord do that which is good in his sight" (I Chronicles 19:13).

"BEHAVE OURSELVES VALIANTLY"--a needed action today. What does *valiantly* mean? It means stouthearted, powerful, courageous, boldly brave; the opposite being fainthearted. He said, "Let's behave ourselves." It is time to act right while the flood of evil tries to crush everything in its pathway. We should stand strong, for with God on our side, everything is going to turn out alright.

How can you have courage? Hope in God and not in yourself. "Be of good courage, and *he* shall strengthen your heart, all ye that hope in the Lord" (Psalm 31:24). It is in the eyes, mind, and heart. Look up to God. Fasten your mind on the Word and let not your heart be troubled, neither be afraid.

Speak courage! You are what you speak.

They helped every one his neighbour; and every one said to his brother, Be of good courage, So the car-

131

penter encouraged the goldsmith, and he that smootheth with the hammer him that smote the anvil...Fear thou not; for I am with thee: be not dismayed; for I am thy God: I will strengthen thee; yea, I will help thee; yea, I will uphold thee with the right hand of my righteousness. For I the Lord thy God will hold thy right hand, saying unto thee, Fear not; I will help thee (Isaiah 41:6-7,10,13).

What are you doing to speak courage? What do you talk about in the coffee shop? What do you talk about on the telephone? What is it you are spreading? Is it how bad everything is, or how the Lord will help us if we will lean upon Him? Where is our confidence? Is it in a system or in the Lord? "Some trust in chariots, and some in horses: but we will remember the name of our God" (Psalm 20:7). What is our faith in, and what kind of spirit are we spreading? Is it one of hope or hopelessness, courage or fear?

Live well, full of courage, for you influence others. Booker T. Washington said, "No man can hold another man in the gutter without remaining there himself." I say, "No man can spread courage without lifting both out of the gutter." What are we leaving the next generation? What kind of cathedrals of the heart are we building? What concepts, principles, and spirits are they catching from us? What is it we are building? The following poem says it well.

THE BRIDGE BUILDER
Will Allen Dromgoole

An old man going a lone highway
Came at the evening, cold and gray,
To a chasm vast and wide and steep,
With waters rolling cold and deep.
The old man crossed in the twilight dim,
The sullen stream had no fears for him;
But he turned when safe on the other side,
And built a bridge to span the tide.

"Old man," said a fellow pilgrim near,
"You are wasting your strength with building here.
Your journey will end with the ending day,
You never again will pass this way.
You've crossed the chasm, deep and wide,
Why build you this bridge at eventide?"

The builder lifted his old gray head.
"Good friend, in the path I have come," he said,
"There followeth after me today
A youth whose feet must pass this way.
The chasm that was as nought to me
To that fair-haired youth may a pitfall be;
He, too, must cross in the twilight dim--
Good friend, I am building this bridge for him."

No man is an island. What you are affects your generation. "For none of us liveth to himself, and no man dieth

to himself" (Romans 14:7). Are we giving each other and those following in our footsteps courage and faith? Or are we giving them questions and doubt? Do we know our God so we can be strong and do exploits? What are we? What do we speak and how do we act?

It is time for leaders, fathers, mothers, teachers and ministers in America to take courage and stand for right.

And when Asa heard these words, and the prophecy of Oded the prophet, he took courage, and put away the abominable idols out of all the land of Judah and Benjamin, and out of the cities which he had taken from Ephraim, and renewed the altar of the Lord, that was before the porch of the Lord (II Chronicles 15:8).

Who has the courage to renew the altar of the Lord? Who has the courage to buck the tide of evil? Is there anyone that will join the army of the Lord and do something instead of sigh behind his closed doors? False doctrines, Satanism, and Eastern cults are bold about their beliefs--how can the church be any different when we have the real power? Where is the courage of David that faced Goliath and said, "I come to you in the name of the Lord!"? Are we afraid? Do we feel like the battle is too great? Is it too far gone? With God all things are possible. Take courage, go forth to stand strong, for the battle is the Lord's. He is the Captain, and He always wins.

Andrew Jackson said, "One man with courage makes a majority." This was proven in the case of David, Daniel, Joseph, and Esther. Cervantes said, "He that loses wealth loses much, but he that loses courage loses all." Be strong and of good courage, for with courage you will make it victorious to the end. Be courageous and give courage to others. Lady Diana Cooper wrote these words about Winston Churchill: "When I said that the best thing he had done was to give the people courage, he answered, 'I never gave them courage; I was able to focus theirs.' " Courage just never gives up! It fights until the victory comes. That is what is needed today in a world filled with heinous crimes, where people's value systems have gone awry. We will stand for right, even if it is not the popular thing to do.

As an unknown writer wrote, "It takes courage to say 'No!' squarely to evil when all those around you are saying, 'Yes.' It takes courage to speak the truth when, by a little twisting, you can gain some advantage or escape punishment. It takes courage to face slander and lies, and to carry yourself with cheerfulness, grace, and dignity for a long while before the lie can be corrected." Yes, it takes courage to be strong, and to choose the way of excellence, but it is worth it!

Section IV

EXCELLENCE

Excellence means the quality of being excellent; superior, first claass, of great worth; eminently good; synonymous with worthy, choice, prime, valuable, select, exquisite.

This section deals with the second Mile Principle, as well as the opposite of excellent giving.

On Lincoln's birthday an intersting cartoon appeared in a newspaper. It showed a small log cabin at the base of a mountain, and the White House at the top of the mountain. A ladder connected the two buildings. At the bottom of the cartoon were these words: "The ladder is still there!" To climb that ladder, however, means sweat and toil.

The way of excellence is before us, but to get there takes hard work and discipline. We choose either excellence, or second best. My prayer is that every reader will choose the superior way!

Chapter 15

GIVING BEYOND

This is the second mile principle: Jesus said, "And whosoever shall compel thee to go a mile, go with him twain" (Matthew 5:41). Doing more than is required is the road to fulfillment and true greatness. He that does only enough to get by will always taste the dust in his mouth. He will never know the fresh air that is reserved only on the mountaintop. The one who goes over and beyond is the most blessed person in the world.

Across the desert went the servant for his master. He was on an important mission: to get a bride for the son of his master. When he arrived at the city of Nahor feeling hot, sticky, dirty, and tired he went to the well of water. He sat down and waited for the damsels to come. He looked and saw one that was fair to look upon and he ran towards her and asked,

Let me, I pray thee, drink a little water of thy pitcher. And she said, Drink, my lord: and she hasted, and let down her pitcher upon her hand, and gave him drink.

And when she had done *giving* him drink, she said, I will draw water for thy camels also, until they have done drinking. And she hasted, and emptied her pitcher into the trough, and ran again unto the well to draw water, and drew for all his camels (Genesis 24:17-20).

Rebekah could have recoiled from the hot disheveled stranger, but she gave willingly and gave more than was required of her. She was not ignorant to the ways of the desert. She knew how much work it would be to water those camels. A camel is known as the ship of the desert and can drink up to five gallons of water on a hot summer day. It took a long time for her to fill those camels.

Because Rebekah gave, a whole nation was blessed; not only the nation, but Rebekah was blessed. Fortunate, indeed, is the community that has individuals who go through life curing sorrows, healing enmities, sweetening bitter fountains, and scattering happiness and good-will. One such nature can influence an entire community, just as one flower will crowd a room with sweet odors.

The Story of the Spring by the Side of the Road, taken from the hundred-year-old book, *Conquests*, shows what can happen when people decide to give more than is required. This couple did not have to do what they did, but they were motivated by a spirit of giving and because of it, a world was blessed--blessed by the poem that came from the encounter:

A Stranger made his way down a road leading into a wide, expansive, fertile valley. It was late in August, hot, sultry and dusty. The Stranger was weary with the journey and was hungry and thirsty. He wondered where he might find a well or spring, a place to rest and be refreshed.

As he made his way down the road he saw nailed to a tree a sign. On this sign was an arrow, pointing to a path that led back from the road. Beneath the arrow were the words, "To the spring," evidently written by some trembling hand.

Welcome word, "To the spring!" So the Stranger wended his way down the path to where he found a great gushing spring pouring forth from beneath huge jagged rocks. All around about this wonderful spring were mammoth oak trees growing in their luxuriance. Beneath the spring was a pool of water made by the falling of the stream. There were cups by the side of the spring. The underbrush had all been cleared away. Near the spring a rustic seat had been builded.

The Stranger drank freely from the spring and was refreshed. He took off his coat and his linen and bathed his face, hands and arms in the pool below the spring and was refreshed again. This done he sat down on the rustic seat to rest. From there he beheld what at first he had not seen, a basket of ripe, beautiful apples, hanging to a limb of a tree just over the spring.

On the basket was a sign, evidently written by the same trembling hand that had made the one by the side of the road. The sign read, "Stranger, these apples are yours. Help yourself." He took a couple of fine juicy ones and ate them. O they were so good. As the Stranger sat there rested and refreshed he found himself wondering what in the world this could mean. All this comfort and no one there to collect any nickels or dimes. What could it mean!

The birds were singing their evening songs. All the air a solemn stillness held. The golden threads of sunlight poured down through the leaves of the trees. What could it all mean?

It finally dawned upon him that there must be someone nearby whose love for humanity and whose unselfish devotion had led them to arrange the wonderful setting of the spring and asked no returns except the sweet satisfaction of having arranged a place where weary travelers might be directed so they could lay down their burdens and be refreshed.

His curiosity was deeply aroused. He wanted to meet persons with such a vision and with such a passion for service and to inquire why all this comfort. He looked for some path which might lead to the explanation. He discovered the path, leading out of the forest trees. He followed it up through the farm yard gate, through the garden gate, up the garden path past the old fashioned flowers, pinks and hollyhocks, to a little old house on the edge of the orchard. After knocking, an old man with a benign face came to the door. "Good evening, Stranger, good evening, come in. Come right in," he said in that good old fashioned, hospitable spirit.

"Neighbor, I've called to ask about the story of the spring. Can you tell me the story of the spring down by the side of the road?"

"O, it's the story of the spring you are after, is it?" the old man said as he laughed the deep laugh that came from the depths of his great generous soul. "The Story of the Spring. Excuse me please, Stranger, and I will call Mother. She loves to tell the Story of the Spring."

Having called the old Mother she came in, sat down, folded over her gingham apron to cover up the spots, as you have seen your Mother and I have seen mine do so many times when a stranger happened in. "The Story of the Spring is it, Stranger? You are asking for the Story of the Spring?"

Brushing away a tear and swallowing a lump that came in her throat, for it was a tender story she was to tell, she proceeded.

"It was this way, Stranger. Fifty years ago Father and I were sweethearts together. Frequently we would take long walks in the moonlight after the day's work was done. On these walks we would dream of how we would invest our lives for others. Sometimes we would think how interesting it would be to give the world a song it might go singing down life's weary way. Sometimes we would wonder if the time would ever come when we could give the world a book that might cheer, instruct, encourage and gladden humanity with all its burdens, heartaches and struggles. And sometimes we would dream of a possible time when we might have piles of gold with which we might help the ambitious, relieve the distressed and render such blessed service as we observed humanity so much needed.

"All these thoughts seemed but vain dreams for we were poor young people, shut away from educational advantages, necessary to so ambitious a dream, so we decided that we were never to be permitted to give the world a song, or a book, or never to have the piles of gold; we would do the next greatest thing, make a home that might be a help and an inspiration making other homes great and worth while for after all, great homes count as the nation's greatest assets.

"The years were repining and so we were married. The immediate question was, 'Where was the home to be located?' Father at once began to look about for a strategic location for such a home. He found this wide, expansive, fertile valley. Here we knew that we would be finally surrounded with many homes, the setting of our dream.

"So Father filed on this claim as a homestead. The evening he came home with the papers we came to this spot and kneeled down upon the sod and dedicated the quarter to be God's acre for service. We soon cut away the timber with which to build our house. We added an extra room as our guest chamber. Father proceeded to clear the farm and put out the orchard.

"We would listen for the settlers driving in with their ox wagons. At the sound of the rumbling of these wagons Father or I would go down to the valley road and ask the settlers to come in for the night. Father helped them locate their homesteads, then rally the neighbors to help roll up their log cabins. Loving service was the word, the passion of our hearts. Many a young family found the Savior about our family altar.

"So, Stranger, for fifty years now, Father and I have lived for the people of the valley. We have shared with them all our joys. We have been by their sides as they have needed our help. We have loved their children and sought to inspire them to become useful and great for their country. Our little brood has come up and mingled with the children of the valley. We have seen swarms of these blessed young lives come up through these beautiful years.

"They have completed their work here in school and have gone out to the Colleges and Universities for life's further training, have come back to the valley for the final touches of the atmosphere of the valley and multitudes have gone out to the ends of the earth to mingle in service for humanity and to serve their country's flag.

"So for fifty years now, Stranger, Father and I have lived for the people of the valley and have beautifully realized our dream. But one day I was coming in from the garden and found Father sitting by the fireplace crying. I said, 'What in the world are you crying for, Dad?'

" 'When I saw you down in the garden this morning, Mother, with your face so pale, your hair so white, your shoulders so rounded by the burdens you have borne by my side these fifty years and when I saw you come up the garden path so trembly and faltering like, I could not keep the tears back and found myself saying, 'Never again, never again, never again will Mother and I have strength to smooth the pillows of the dying through the long, weary nights. Never again will we be able to load the flour, hams, and potatoes into the wagon or sleigh and take relief to the poor and the suffering.' I am not crying, Mother, because we are getting old. Heaven never beckoned with a sweeter call than now, but it was such a joy to go out by your side, Mother, and minister to the people of the valley that my heart is hungry to go right on and on with this blessed work. So when I saw you this morning, Mother, looking so frail I realized how nearly our race was run. It is from heart hunger that I am crying, Mother.'

"So," she said, "I sat down and cried by his side and we talked it all over. Finally I said, 'Father, let's do one more fine service for humanity before the touch of Time shall palsy our hands utterly. Let's do what we have been thinking of doing so many years. Rest good Father, and sharpen your ax and take plenty of time and cut away the underbrush from about the spring. Build a rustic seat. Cut a path through to the road. God will hang the boughs of our apple trees full of apples every year. I'll take my old trembly hands and, as best I can, fix up the signs and then we will render this last expression of our love to God and our fellow travelers down life's rugged way.'

"When it was all done, while the caroling birds accompanied us with their evening symphony, we dedicated the Spring to God and humanity, asking no return except the sweet satisfaction that we had rendered one more service to our fellow man and made it possible for him to turn aside from this dusty weary way, find a place of quiet, find refreshment and rest and a place to lay down his burden and in sweet meditations catch the spirit of the Valley."

Little did those old people realize that this stranger was none less than the great American poet, Sam Foss. When he heard this story he went out and wrote the poem that has gone around the world, entitled, *The House By the Side of the Road and Being a Friend of Man.*

Wherever the presence of Jesus is there is a growing passion to serve. The real mark of greatness is a passion to serve. As Jesus said, "He that would be greatest among you, let him be servant of all."

A score of years ago a young woman missionary to the Congo region in the heart of Africa was returning to her homeland on furlough. Every detail of her trip had been arranged and her baggage was even put on board the streamer on which she was to sail when she was suddenly stricken with Congo fever. She died in a few hours.

Found among her belongings when her trunk was opened was her Bible. On the inside cover drawn in beautiful characters and with different-colored inks was this poem written by George Macdonald:

I said, "Let me walk in the field."
He said, "No walk in the town."
I said, "There are no flowers there."
He said, "No flowers, but a crown."

I cried, "But the skies are black,
There is nothing but noise and din."
And He wept as He sent me back,
"There is more," He said, "There is sin."

I said, "But the air is thick,
And fogs are veiling the sun."
He answered, "Yet souls are sick,
And souls in the dark undone."

I said, "I shall miss the light,
And friends will miss me, they say."
He answered, "Choose tonight
If I am to miss you, or they."

I pleaded for time to be given,
He said, "Is it hard to decide?
It will not seem so hard in heaven
To have followed the steps of your Guide."

Then into His hand went mine;
And into my heart came He;
And I walk in a light divine,
The path I had feared to see.

It is said of this woman that the natives of the Congo
simply adored her; her consecration, her purity of life and
her personal love for them made her a queen among them.
She earned this position. She gave of her life, substance,
and spirit. She epitomized the going beyond what is required, and because of it reaped many souls for the
kingdom.

One night in the East End of London a young doctor
was turning out the lights of a mission hall in which he was
working. He found a ragged boy hiding in a dark corner,

where he begged to be allowed to sleep. The doctor took the homeless boy to his own room, fed him and tried to get his story. He learned that the boy was living in a coal bin with a number of other boys. He persuaded the boy to show him where these boys were. They went through narrow alleys and finally came to a hole in the wall of a factory. "Look in there," he said. The doctor struck a match and looked around, crawling into the cellar.

Finally he found thirteen boys with only bits of old burlap to protect them from the cold. One lad was clasping to him a four-year-old brother. All were sound asleep. The doctor caught a vision then and there of service for his Lord. He cared for those boys and started the Bernardo Homes for neglected children. At the time of the death of Dr. Bernardo, the newspapers reported that he had taken and surrounded with a Christian atmosphere over 80,000 homeless boys and girls.

He did not have to do what he did, but he had the second mile principle in him. When you are faced with an opportunity to do good, what will you do with it? Will you walk on by as the priest in the story of the good Samaritan, or will you go beyond what is required? The world is hurting and crying for those who will not only see, but care enough to do something about it. What can you do? What are you doing? If you help one, you are doing better than nothing. Do something, but give yourself to the higher way which is going beyond.

Going beyond is doing something to help someone without worrying about being paid for it. In New Jersey a man who lived by the side of a great national highway was seen out in the thoroughfare filling up a small hole. "Only took me a minute," he said, "and I probably saved hundreds of dollars for the motorists who went by, as well as something for the state. It just needed to be done, and I wasn't busy." And that man does not own a car himself.

Find something to do today that will enrich the lives of others, whether it is taking care of homeless children or filling in a hole in the highway. Do something! Great or small does not matter. "Whatsoever thy hand findeth to do, do it with thy might; for there is no work, nor device, nor knowledge, nor wisdom, in the grave, whither thou goest" (Ecclesiastes 9:10). You are going to die, he is saying, and when you do, it is all over. So you might as well give your best to life while you are living and bless others, as well as yourself.

Chapter 16

SECOND CLASS ATTITUDE: "GIVE ME"

When one is concerned only about himself, he will eventually die within. Greed, envy, pride and selfishness grow within the heart of a man that seeks only his own way. He cannot stand for another to succeed because it was not him. He is eaten up with envy. The Grecian story is told about a man who killed himself through envy. His fellow citizens had reared a statue to one of their number who was a celebrated victor in the public games. So strong was the feeling of envy which this incited in the breast of one of the hero's rivals that he went forth every night in order, if possible, to destroy that monument. After repeated efforts he moved it from its pedestal, and it fell, but in its fall it crushed him.

How like the little boy that said to his sister one day when they were both on the rocking horse together, "If one of us would get off there would be more room for me." And like the little girl that was concerned only with her world. The teacher took the first grade class to a dairy where a guide showed the children through the entire plant, explaining the whole process. The tour over, the guide asked if anyone had a question. The little girl raised her hand.

"Did you notice," she asked, "that I've got on my new snow suit?"

Completely oblivious to everything about her, all she thought of was herself. Many times we are this way. Anything that concerns us we are interested in. Our church, our home, our kids, our clothes, our car becomes what we like to talk about. When people are talking and someone tells a story about their grandmother, we immediately think of a story to tell about our grandmother. We relate to other people with things that concern us. It is time to break out of the mold and care for things and people that are beyond our own circle. Get out of the rut of normalcy, and reach for those that are hurting and in need.

This chapter on seeing only our needs is placed at the end in the section of Excellence. Excellence is first-class or superior. Some people are content to choose second-class and put up with every bump, when they could just as well go first-class.

There was a man in the Bible that had this second-class attitude. He has already been mentioned once. His name was King Ahab. Notice what he said and how it got him in trouble.

And Ahab spake unto Naboth, saying, *Give me* thy vineyard, that I may have it for a garden of herbs, because it is near unto my house: and I will give thee for it a better vineyard than it; or, if it seem good to thee, I will give thee the worth of it in money. And Naboth said to Ahab, The Lord forbid it me, that I should give the inheritance of my fathers unto thee (I Kings 21:2-3).

When Ahab went home he was very heavy and displeased, so he laid down on the bed, turned his face to the wall and would not eat. When his wife, Jezebel, came in the room, she asked, "Why are you so sad?"

He said, "Naboth the Jezreelite will not give me his vineyard." So wicked Jezebel started scheming. She brought about Naboth's death with Ahab's help and then Ahab got the vineyard. But his "give me" attitude got him more than the vineyard. Selfishness always brings judgement.

Elijah enters the scene. The Lord told him to go down and talk to Ahab about his illegal scheme to obtain something that was not rightfully his. He also told him to tell Ahab that in the place where the dogs licked Naboth's blood, they would also lick his blood. He also had a word for Jezebel. He said the dogs would eat her by the wall of Jezreel.

Did it happen? When God says it, it always happens. Ahab disguised himself in battle, but a certain man drew a bow at a venture and smote the king between the joints of the harness. When Ahab died they washed out the chariot by the pool of Samaria and the dogs licked up his blood, just as the Lord had spoken.

God does not forget. Later on, Jezebel painted her face, looked out a window and the eunuchs threw her down to the ground, where Jehu trod on her with the horses. After he had eaten and drunk, he told them to go bury the cursed woman. When they went to bury her, all they could find was the skull, the feet and the palms of her hands. Her hands that had shed innocent blood were lying detached from her body on the bloody dirt as a reminder that a "give me" attitude which harms another always loses.

There is nothing wrong with wanting a blessing, and we should desire to be blessed. In all our getting, though, we need to think of God and others, and not only think of ourselves. When Jacob was blessed of God, he did not forget the Lord. He had a visitation from the Lord and took a stone and said, "...of all that thou shalt give me I will surely give the tenth unto thee" (Genesis 28:22). He did not forget where his blessings came from.

The motive for us saying "Give me" must be examined. If it is motivated by selfishness, greed, or spite, then it becomes a curse to us instead of a blessing.

A lady who had a hatred of a certain man and caused his death spoke the same words that Ahab spoke. When Salome, the daughter of Herodias, danced before the wine-filled king, he was stirred to the point of offering her anything she wanted. He said, "Ask of me whatsoever thou wilt, and I will give it thee" (Mark 6:22).

Can you imagine such an opportunity? When she ran to her mother and inquired of her what she should ask for, her mother spoke diabolical but astonishing words. When Salome went into the king she said, "...I will that thou *give me* by and by in a charger the head of John the Baptist" (Mark 6:25).

What was the end of Herodias? Since she was the source of Herod's sin, Herodias also became the source of his shame. According to Josephus, Herodias' ambition was Herod's ruin. Jealous of the power of Agrippa her brother, she prodded Herod to demand of Caligula, the emperor, the title of the king. Agrippa saw to it that this demand was refused, and Herod was banished and ended his days in shame and exile. The pride of Herodias forced her to be faithful to her husband in the disgrace and misfortune she herself had caused.

From Genesis to Revelation, all deeds done receive a reaping. Revelation brings us to the awareness that there is a day coming when all will be judged. "...and they were judged every man according to their works" (Revelation 20:13). He also says, "And, behold, I come quickly; and my reward is with me, to give every man according as his work shall be" (Revelation 22:12).

This is the time now to judge ourselves, and plan ahead for that day. "For if we would judge ourselves, we should not be judged" (I Corinthians 11:31). Self-judgment avoids chastisement. If neglected, the Lord judges, and the result is chastisement. That is now, but at the end of time, there will be no chastisement; it will be judgment.

As we come to the end of the book, we can ask ourselves, "Am I giving all that I can give? What are my motives in seeking what I'm seeking? Am I giving in a proper attitude? Am I being a good steward of all that the Lord has given me?" So many questions to ask ourselves, but we must always keep growing or we will stagnate. This is the day to grow and become, and not settle for less. Whatever you give into life, it will pay you back. Whatever you invest into heaven's bank account will pay rich dividends. You establish the return by how much you put in. The old poem says it well:

I bargained with Life for a penny,
And Life would pay no more,
However I begged at evening
When I counted my scanty store.

For Life is a just employer,
He gives you what you ask,
But once you have set the wages,
Why, you must bear the task.

I worked for a menial's hire,
Only to learn, dismayed,
That any wage I had asked of Life,
Life would have willingly paid.

We can give and it shall be given, or we can withhold and it shall be withheld. The choice is up to us how much we give. What will it be, cursing or blessing? Today is a blank piece of paper. You will write the rest of your life starting today, so write well. I would like to leave you with a little reading that has inspired me through the years. It says, "Refuse to open your purse, and soon you cannot open your sympathy. Refuse to give, and soon you will cease to enjoy that which you have. Refuse to love, and you lose the power to love and be loved. Withhold your affections and you become a moral paralytic. But the moment you open wider the door of your life, you let the sunshine of your life into some soul, and it reflects back on you."

Chapter 17

A MORE EXCELLENT WAY

After having talked about the nine gifts of the spirit, Paul tells the Corinthian church that there is something superior to even the gifts. He says, "But covet earnestly the best gifts: and yet shew I unto you a more excellent way" (I Corinthians 12:31).

"Though I speak with the tongues of men and of angels, and have not charity, I am become as sounding brass, or a tinkling cymbal" (I Corinthians 13:1). He told them if they had all the gifts, all the faith, and gave all their goods to feed the poor, but were not motivated to do those things by love, then it profited them nothing. It was all in vain!

Let us not get the cart before the horse. Our motivation to give to God and to others must be love. If we struggle with these things, then we need to be baptized with love. What is love? God is love! And God so loved that He gave. Breaking it down into our terms, love is many things.

Webster tells us it is a feeling of strong personal attachment induced by that which delights or commands admiration, by sympathetic understanding, or by ties of kinship;

ardent affection. What does this say to you? It says to me that if I am to love the poor, love to give, and love to obey the commandments, then I must get a kinship with God. I must have a deep affection for Him and seek to delight myself in the things of the Lord.

As an outgrowth of my love for Him, then I will do the following, for this is what love really is--I Corinthians 13-style:

1. I will be patient with people.
2. I will be kind.
3. I will not brag on myself, or become puffed up.
4. I will behave myself so as not to embarrass others.
5. I will not seek my own selfish way, but His way.
6. I will keep my temper and not become upset easily.
7. I will determine to think no evil.
8. I will not rejoice in the sins of others.
9. I will rejoice in truth and righteousness.
10. I will bear all things gracefully.
11. I will believe all things, and not be cynical.
12. I will hope for the best in all things.
13. I will endure all things with God's grace.

Proverbs 17:27 says, "...A man of understanding is of an excellent spirit." It is my duty to understand the ways of God, and to do them, if I want His blessings. What are His ways? What did Jesus teach to the people? He often rebuked the religious leaders, the priests, or the ministry. When He talked to those considered the common folk He was more patient. In fact, they thronged Him. He always had a crowd around Him. The reason they turned against Him was because the smug, hateful, self-righteous, jealous priests and Pharisees incited the people against Him with lies. People always follow leaders, and their leaders were sure not in touch with God.

Jesus forgave a harlot, He gave a tax-collector mercy and attention, and He gave His precious time to a woman of ill-repute that had been married at least five times. He was very kind to those that did not profess to have the truth, but those that professed to be righteous and learned in the scriptures, He scathingly rebuked. "But woe unto, Pharisee! for ye tithe...and pass over judgment and the *LOVE* of God: these ought ye to have done, and not to leave the other undone" (Luke 11:42). Jesus is saying you should tithe, but that is not enough. You must love God and one another.

And what did He tell the people? He told them:

1. Love your enemies (Matthew 5:44).
2. Love thy neighbor as thyself (Matthew 19:19).
3. Love the Lord thy God with all thy heart, and with all thy soul and with all thy mind, and with all thy strength (Mark 12:30). He never will accept second-best. He never has from the beginning of time, and He is not going to start in this lax generation.
4. These things I command you, That ye love one another! (John 15:17).
5. If ye love me feed my sheep (John 21:17). Notice: LOVE ALWAYS GIVES.

When Jesus told them to love God with all their heart and to love their neighbor as themselves, a scribe answered Him in such a way that Jesus told him that he was not far from the kingdom of God. What did the scribe say? "And to love him with all the heart, and with all the understanding, and with all the soul, and with all the strength, and to love his neighbour as himself, is more than all whole burnt-offerings and sacrifices" (Mark 12:33). Jesus in so many words said, "You are beginning to understand what I am saying to you. You are not far from the kingdom. You are getting close." Jesus said, "By this shall all men know that ye are my disciples, if ye have love one to another" (John 13:35). Paul said, "Love worketh no ill towards his neighbor: therefore love is the fulfilling of the law" (Romans 13:10).

Many are concerned about the law. The fulfilling of the law is to love as the description above. Everything else is void. Without love we will not inherit eternal life. I think all of us need to work on getting more love into our hearts, ways, and attitudes.

John said it so beautifully:

Beloved, let us love one another: for love is of God, and every one that loveth is born of God, and knoweth God. He that loveth not, knoweth not God: for God is love. If we love one another, God dwelleth in us, and his love is perfected in us. If a man say, I love God, and hateth his brother, he is a liar: (I John 4:7-8,12,20).

We are so close to the end of time, it is now imperative that we search our hearts and make ourselves ready for the bridegroom, for all liars shall have their part in the lake of fire (Revelation 21:8). My prayer is, "God, help us to tear down the walls between us. Those that have lied in order to lift themselves up, may they repent and make it right. Help us to humble ourselves and quit slashing each other. Let us love not only in word, but in deed. Cleanse us from the deception of hate, evil speaking, and the justification of spiritual gossip that has crept among Your children. Wash us and make us clean within. Help us to keep the laws of purity and holiness without the taint of self-righteousness, for there is none righteous except Thee, O God! Help us, O Lord, for we are a desperate people living in a desperate generation. We desire to have Your power flow through us, but we obstruct it with our lack of love. Help us to love as You loved, seventy times seven every day, and pray the prayer of forgiveness You prayed. Let us not be bitter or hold grudges toward those that have wronged us, but let us put on Christ and love with the unsearchable love of God. Let it burn out all fleshly carnal thoughts until we are a transparent mirror of Thy holiness and love. Be it done this day, O magnificent God! Amen."

It is time to cleanse our ways and get the upward and outward look. The upward looks to Jesus; the outward wants to help others. This is the day to give not only money, goods, and assistance to people, it is time to give them Jesus. If people have Jesus, they have everything. Jesus told the twelve disciples, "Heal the sick, cleanse the lepers, raise the dead, cast out devils; freely ye have received, freely give" (Matthew 10:8).

In April, I was sitting in the Tri-city airport in Tennessee with my Bible open on my lap. We had been instructed to get off the plane and wait until further word from the Atlanta airport, so I was just waiting and reading. An older man walked by me, glanced at my Bible, walked on past, and then turned around and came back and said, "Is that the Bible you are reading?" I said, "Yes. This is my favorite book."

He said, "Would you come into that coffee shop with me and talk to me about God and the Bible?"

I saw two of our ministers in there, Revs. Jesse Williams and James Tharp, so I said, "I'll be glad to talk to you about the Lord and the Bible."

We went in and sat down next to the table where the two ministers were, and we began to talk about God. After he told me he was on the way to the Veterans hospital because of a serious illness, I told him about some of the miracles that had been happening recently and how God wanted to heal him and fill him with His spirit. Then I asked him, "Do you mind if we pray for you right now?" He said, "No, I would be glad to have you pray."

I called over to the ministers who were sitting there, introduced the man, told them his need, and asked them to help me pray for the gentleman. Come to find out, Brother Williams was from the area where the man was going. He said he would follow through and send someone to minister to the man in the hospital. Isn't God awesome? We prayed, and not long after I was on the plane back to California.

I gave the man Jesus, but had not heard what happened to him. Then in July a card came in the mail. It was from the man we had prayed for in the airport. These were his words:

> We met sometime ago at the Tri-cities airport. There you introduced me to Brother Williams of Fayetteville, and also a Brother Tharp. The three of you prayed for me. Thank you, Jesus, for the three of you. Roy Barnhill of Lumberton allowed me to borrow his copy of your book, *When Ye Pray*. I read it through almost without stopping. It has already helped me. If we never meet again this side of heaven, I plan to see you there. Agape, *J.G.*

As I read the card, tears of gratitude ran down my cheeks. As I praised the Lord, I also prayed, "God, please, help me to be more sensitive to the needs of others. How many more people are out there who need someone to take the time to give them Jesus? Oh, God, take away all my pride and intimidations. Help me to help people and give them what they really need, and that is You."

Let us live the more excellent way, the way of love. When we give Jesus, we give love, for He is love. Jesus said, "Freely give." Let His love flow from us and through us like a river to a thirsty, hurting world. Let us lift Him up and give hope to hungry hearts.

He and He alone is excellent! We must work toward the more excellent way! The following scriptures describe His excellency:

Touching the Almighty, we cannot find him out: he is *excellent in power...* (Job 37:23).

O Lord, our Lord, how *excellent* is thy name in all the earth! who hast set his glory above the heavens (Psalm 8:1).

Let them praise the name of the Lord: for his name alone is *excellent,* his glory is above the earth and heaven (Psalm 148:13).

Praise him for his mighty acts: praise him according to his *excellent* greatness (Psalm 150:2).

Sing unto the Lord; for he hath done *excellent* things (Isaiah 12:5).

This is the day to become aware of His excellence! Let it fill our hearts and minds, for His excellence is based in love. This day let us get our hearts right and give unto the Lord all that is due Him: ourselves, our tithes, offerings, worship, witness, or anything He asks of us. "Give unto the Lord the glory due unto his name: bring an offering, and come before him: worship the Lord in the beauty of holiness" (I Chronicles 16:29). He promised us blessings when we follow His plan, but more than financial blessings are the riches of glory that far outweigh temporal things. Let us seek the way above and we will be taken care of sufficiently and abundantly by our magnificent God! Choose this day the more excellent way.

Let me leave you with this scripture which the angels, the elders, and the four beasts say unto the Lord, and which we should also say to bless the Lord daily: "Blessing, and glory, and wisdom, and thanksgiving, and honour, and power, and might, be unto our God for ever and ever, Amen" (Revelation 7:12).

EPILOGUE

MY HIGH RESOLVE:

I hereby dedicate my heart to the ministry of compassion. Realizing how few care what the burdens, heartaches, struggles or troubles of humanity may be I shall give my life to sympathy, to love for the unlovely, and to make every life over which I may have an influence, more endurable and interesting.

I resolve to take time to be a great heart: to be on the lookout for people perplexed, unfortunate, distressed, disheartened and discouraged.

I would be as my Master, "moved with compassion." I resolve to give ear to the cry of pain, misfortune and sorrow. To me may come those weighed down with the burdens of life. I shall not shun scenes of anguish. I will go where the wayfarer has fallen among thieves. I will not pass by on the other side.

I deeply resolve to live a life that shall be like "a great rock in a weary land." Tender with sympathy, sweetened by a deep love for my fellows in trouble, I resolve to be one who really cares.

It shall be my high endeavor to be the channel through which shall flow blessings in every direction.

I shall keep my pitcher filled at the fountain of truth and pour cups full for the thirsty ones by the wayside.

I resolve that my life will become as music to others. My life is like a keyboard. If I let the Master's fingers sweep over it, a weary world will catch notes of melody, for the life that is in tune with God is keyed to the note of love.

Love will be the scepter with which I rule my world. I resolve to pour my life into the worthy cause of the kingdom of God, and to love Him first, and others as myself. I will give and give, so that I might truly live.